REDEFINE
YOURSELF

About the Author

Michael is the former fitness expert on NBC's *The Biggest Loser* /MSN Chicago tour. The owner of a successful Chicago personal training business, his fitness and life-structure programs have helped his clients lose more than 2,500 pounds since 2005. Michael has been featured in *Muscle & Fitness* and *Today's Chicago Woman* magazines, among others. During his time as the official trainer for PBS's *The Whitney Reynolds Show*, he also produced an inspirational segment about his travels in Guatemala.

Having researched emotion and coping behaviors in university-level studies, Michael has presented various fitness, motivation, body image, and stress-management programs at Illinois State University, DePaul University, corporations, high schools, and workshops.

Redefine Yourself:
The Simple Guide to Happiness

"Inspiring in its simple yet meaningful message, this book is an important reminder of the power of the mind. By simply using our thoughts as tools working for us rather than weapons against us, Michael shows us how we can truly learn to live out our best lives."

—DANA MICHELLE COOK,
Emmy Award winner and producer of *The Empowerment Project*

"From mindfulness to changing your routines, this book has what you need to take a good look at yourself and start making changes that will work for you. Michael is honest about the fact that while change isn't necessarily easy, it's attainable if you are disciplined, insightful, and perseverant. With the information on these pages, you can truly change your life!"

—TORI NYBERG,
LPC of Elevate Performance Counseling

"Highly recommended! Michael takes all of his research and distills the information in a relatable way. He also sets you up for success by outlining how to keep life simple, be in the moment, and always bring your life back to your purpose."

—CARRIE KENNEDY,
founder and executive producer of *Chicago Ideas Week*

"An empowering go-to guide for actively seeking your life's desires! This book sheds light on how our very own behavior affects the outcomes to our goals. Read, redefine yourself, repeat!"

—HOLLY STUBNAR, M.S.
Board Certified Behavior Analyst

REDEFINE YOURSELF

The Simple Guide to Happiness

MICHAEL MOODY

Ainsley Press
Chicago

This book is not intended as a substitute for the advice of physicians, psychologists, or other medical professionals. The reader should regularly consult a physician in matters relating to his/her health and particularly with respect to any symptoms that may require diagnosis or medical attention.

Ainsley Press, Publisher
Editor: Andrew Elsass
Cover Design: Jasmine Ojeda
Format: Maureen Cutajar

Publisher's Cataloging-in-Publication
Moody, Michael, 1979-
      Redefine yourself : the simple guide to happiness /
Michael Moody. -- First edition.
      pages cm
      Includes bibliographical references.
      LCCN 2015931847
      ISBN-10: 0-9863527-0-5
      ISBN-13: 978-0-9863527-0-6
      1. Self-realization. 2. Health. 3. Happiness.
I. Title.
BF637.S4M636 2015   58.1   QBI15-600027

Ainsley Press books are available for special promotions and premiums. For details contact: info@ainsleypress.com.

I dedicate this book to my family, friends, and clients who remind me that life is always bigger than the moment.

Acknowledgements

OVER THREE YEARS AGO I told my great friend Melissa Garvey that I wanted to write a book. Instead of asking why, she said, "How can I help you?" Her support and enthusiasm are the reasons why this book exists today. I only hope that everyone can have the same kind of person in their life when pursuing a goal.

There are many others, including Sammy Ojeda, Carol Lewke, Sherry Hoel, Tim Sieges, Craig Beggs, Cheryl Beggs, and Dana Cook, who always gave the endless support and love needed to finish the daunting task of capturing an idea and sharing it within a book.

Also, I'm fortunate to have trained many people who became my great friends, confidants, and biggest supporters over the last ten years. Adam Weber, Erica Dennison Daitch, Mike Pippenger, Lisa Sabo, Carrie Kennedy, and Joan Schumaker have been wonderful parts of my life and I couldn't be any more thankful for them.

Additionally, I'm especially grateful for the unbelievable editing work of Andrew Elsass, cover design of Jasmine Ojeda, and the rest of my review team who provided constructive feedback during this process. Their contributions were not only an act of support for me, but to all future readers looking for inspiration. Thank you again Pete Alwan, Molly Rabinovitz, Amanda Madsen Niro, Danyel Donahue, Jean Reubner, Chelsea Percoco, Natalie Vina, Amanda Alford, Cindy Rick, Jamar Holloway, Kimberly Flannigan, Rachel Kiernan, Katy Cassata, and Matthew Eaton!

Lastly, I wouldn't be who I am if not for my father, Michael Moody, my brother, Jon Moody, and my grandparents, Don and Geri Moody. They have taught me how to love, live, and push for the best.

Contents

Redefining Yourself with Awareness, Acceptance, and Adaptation

THINK ABOUT YOUR LIFE for a moment. Do you think it is a struggle? Are you generally unhappy? Is something or someone missing? Do you feel out of place?

Whether or not you answered yes to these questions, you are probably reading this book because you are searching for something meaningful in your life, or for a solution to change how you feel or behave.

The *Redefine Yourself* approach will serve as the catalyst for this change. During this transformation process, the primary focus of physical and personal change isn't just nutrition and exercise. It's a targeted focus on awareness, acceptance, and adaptive strategies. Each word is individually significant but most powerful as a sequence.

As you integrate the *Redefine Yourself* approach into your life, you will refine your perspective and understand why you:

- Do what you do.
- Can't reach your goals.
- Find yourself in the same destructive position repeatedly.
- Date the same type of person with or without the same hair color and allow the relationship to last six months to twenty years too long.
- Complain about everything in your life to your friends, who then end up complaining about your complaining, and so forth.
- Can't reach your best physical, emotional, and mental self.
- Live an unhappy and unfulfilled life.

BEGINNING YOUR JOURNEY

Redefine Yourself will help you understand and redefine the very essence of YOU. It is the answer to your perpetual failure to achieve the happiness and success that you desire. You'll uncover your shocking inner self that has undermined your efforts everywhere from the gym to the workplace.

By the end, you'll incorporate the simple approach that will not only reshape your life, but positively impact the people around you. Most important, you will remove the invisible obstructions that hold you back from achieving personal success!

Redefine Yourself will become the "in-your-pocket" resource for daily change. It exemplifies a new generation of health and fitness books that emphasize the mental and emotional "you" when pursuing personal and professional success.

You'll utilize the following three-step process when confronting your inner influences and adapting new strategies:

1. AWARENESS

You are a detective collecting the truth of a moment, observing yourself and every movement, sight, touch, scent, and sound of the world. You are gathering evidence for the truth without judgment. *Redefine Yourself* will help you examine the most common mental and environmental influences on your happiness. This list includes self-talk, surroundings, emotional restraint, fears, insecurities, perceived control, decision-making processes, and belief in your abilities.

You'll probably realize that one could write a separate book about each of these influences. In fact, you'll easily find them in a bookstore or online, already written. But for the purpose of introducing you to you, I've only touched lightly on what you need to think about when examining yourself. We'll call it a light stroke of awareness. At this point, you are just naming what you observe about yourself. While you may not entirely confront the reasons why you're dealing with these challenges, the Redefine Yourself approach will help you accept these challenges and adapt successful strategies to overcome them.

Perhaps you already think that you are fully aware in your daily life. How do you know this? Is this truth based on assumptions or real evidence? Have you separated yourself from your mental judgment and just absorbed the world?

Most people answer no to these questions. You might do this occasionally but not often enough. Instead, you often take a leap of faith without stopping first. You jump, again and again, not knowing where you will land.

You live a forever-looking-forward existence. You pick up bits and pieces around you but never stop the train of life. "Not enough time," you say. However, you make time for things that aren't important to you. "I already know," you say, but have never stopped to look and be certain.

Redefine Yourself isn't the start of a gentle persuasion to do something. It is a knock on the head to make you realize that you're not do-ing something that you think you're doing.

You probably aren't aware as much as you need to be. I know that you've made millions of decisions in your life and have survived thus far. How well have you lived up to this point, however? Could you have lived better if you just halted before reacting? Could you have prevented a disaster by looking in both directions first?

I once wrongly accused my girlfriend of being selfish while she was presenting a gift in her hands. Have you done something similar? I felt hopeless about my direction in life and my inability to change it, but I didn't check to see that the truth was in front of me. Have you, as well?

Redefining yourself means becoming and staying aware. When you dedicate yourself to remaining aware before making a decision, judgment or movement, you are committing to a higher state of living. You are committing to seeing both the real perfections and imperfections of the world.

There is beauty in this awareness. Recently, my girlfriend and I went to a good friend's wedding in Milwaukee. It started with an exchange of rings in the pews of the historic St. Josaphat Basilica and ended in the seventh-floor banquet room of the historic Pfister Hotel in downtown Milwaukee.

The highlight of the evening was the genuine love that I noticed dur-ing the father-of-the-bride's speech. It was unbelievable! I was soaking in the aura of happiness that started in the cathedral eight hours earlier. The guests sincerely loved the couple, and there wasn't a dry eye in the room. It was something special that I captured in that single moment. I always wonder how many of these moments—good and bad—I have missed while distracted with my selfish intentions or focus on my work.

I was not meant to change or add to this wedding moment. It al-ready took motion without me in the picture. I was just a bystander.

There are many more moments, however, which require me to take action. I can make a change to help someone in need, or by removing myself from a situation.

Often, it doesn't matter what leads to a moment. It only matters what you do with it. It requires a fair observation and assessment. This awareness will help you realize the real need to redefine yourself.

2. ACCEPTANCE

When you accept the influences mental and environmental factors have on you, you accept your situation, surroundings, and feelings at that moment. Then, you begin the appropriate adaptive strategies for positive change. You are putting aside your emotional investment and other subconscious influences to start over and redefine you.

Although your focus steers toward your mindset and the environment during a period of awareness, you mustn't dwell on the imperfections of you, your situation, and your surroundings. Additionally, you mustn't fixate on imperfect pieces of life that are unchangeable at the moment. Before adapting new strategies to redefine yourself, you must accept these things in their current state.

Acceptance isn't easy and is a common reason people choose to be less aware of themselves and the world. It took me awhile to understand why people don't stop and "open their eyes." When I did, it made sense: people don't want to. "Ignorance is bliss! The real world stinks!" The world is imperfect, and this is hard to accept. Instead, they construct a rose-colored reality to mask the blight and scathing.

If this is so effective, why are so many people still unhappy? It seems that our instinctive selves always recognize the truth despite our best efforts to ignore it. Our subconscious taps us on the shoulder but doesn't push us over. It just reminds us that it's there and tells us what we should do (even though we don't always do it).

It's our gut barking, and many people are scared to face it at times. They're afraid to identify imperfections in themselves and their environment and new challenges.

Frederick Douglass, a former slave and leader in the abolitionist movement, echoes this in his narratives:

> *"...I would at times feel that learning to read had been a curse rather than a blessing. It had given me a view of my wretched condition, without the remedy. It opened my eyes to the horrible pit, but to no ladder upon which to get out. In moments of agony, I envied my fellow slaves for their stupidity. I often wished myself a beast."*

What an unbelievable quote! Even a man of vigor and ambition like Frederick Douglass questioned being fully aware because of the great truths that he faced.

You may not share the terrible circumstances that Mr. Douglass did as a slave. You're fortunate for this. Nevertheless, there may be an unpleasant reality that might show itself, now or later, when you "open your eyes." To make it worse, you may not know how to handle it or what to do with this new information. You're afraid to recognize that you chose the wrong career, but you depend on it financially. You're scared to accept that you chose the wrong spouse, but you've already raised two kids with him or her.

No matter what action you eventually pursue, you can accept your current situation. You can accept that knowledge is power even though you can't always change it.

What's the point of being aware if you can't always change it then? It helps you understand the world. It helps you understand you. It helps you understand the subtle influences on your behavior, choices, and personality. It helps you recognize what you need to do to be happy.

You're not always given an answer, a path, or the next step when you become aware. Realizing how much you have gained or how isolated you've become because of your job won't be rectified as soon as you notice it.

It's worth knowing, though, in order to achieve a greater purpose: Living a better, happier life. You can't redefine your life without knowing its current shape and accepting it.

Moving forward or redefining yourself can't occur unless you can learn to accept the way a situation is at a given moment. Otherwise, the insight you gain regarding practical decisions and solutions to problems are fruitless.

I struggled with this for a while. I realized that I wouldn't let go of my emotional investment in my personal and professional lives. I wouldn't accept that my marriage wasn't working. I didn't accept that the website design I worked on for two months wasn't right.

Now is the time to trust your instincts, your gut, and your perspective. Put aside your emotional investment and don't be afraid to start over. ACCEPT it and move on. When you don't accept it, tell yourself again and again and again that you should.

3. ADAPTATION

Once you're aware of the challenges you face and you choose to accept them, you are ready to handle your current and unforeseen obstructions to happiness. You will be prepared to adapt your lifestyle and utilize adaptive strategies that apply to multiple facets of your life. The specific solution may be different depending on the situation, but the foundation of your approach won't change. You are just modifying the approach based on new conditions, needs, or wants.

You will also integrate new strategies to practice mindfulness, solve problems, accumulate wisdom through error, create new habits, clarify your purpose, self-police your life, define your boundaries, develop goals to steer positive behavior, and create conversations with others.

Please keep in mind that adaptation means taking action. You are not a bystander in this process. Here are several examples:

Is your friend is a selfish jerk? Accept All-About-Me Julie as she is and ignore her selfish tendencies, discuss how her actions make you feel, or begin dismantling your friendship.

Do you think the president stinks? Accept that the president (insert Republican, Democrat, or Independent here) is the leader of the United States and ignore his political decisions, get involved with politics, or make a grassroots effort for change.

These examples are another way of saying, "Quit complaining and do something." Complaining is primarily an emotional output, the result of boredom or simple conversation lacking any substantial or functional value. On the other hand, adaptation isn't complaining about what you found and sharing how horrible it is for anyone who is or isn't interested in listening. When you develop an evidence-based strategy and choose the best possible decision, you are effectively adapting your life.

REFLECTION SECTIONS

Although reading *Redefine Yourself* is important, taking the time to reflect on YOU is essential for implementing change. I encourage you to take the time to read the questions at the end of most chapters and answer them honestly. Each question will walk you through awareness, acceptance, and adaptation of each influence or area of your life. If you're like me, you'll probably read the questions and think about the answers. Does that mean that you're ready for the next chapter? Absolutely not.

Commit to this journey and don't take the easy way out. You MUST write down your answers. You need these answers for reference later on. Most important, you need to SEE them in front of you. Take the time to write a well-thought out answer and read it. It gives you a chance to see your thoughts written in front of you. It will be very impactful and eye opening.

By the end, you should be able to develop the awareness you've wanted. You will accept the imperfections of life and implement a less stressful lifestyle. It's time to open your mind and begin your journey to redefine yourself.

1

You Are Not Alone

YOU ARE NOT ALONE.

I hope that you find comfort in these words. Before you begin your journey to redefine yourself, I want you to hear about my journey and what led to the creation of this book. You may be able to relate.

My story began with a newfound dedication to redefining myself. Little did I know that the year I devoted to self-exploration would instead be stretched over four years—culminating in a two-week adventure in Guatemala after a couple of years of spiraling uncertainty during my divorce. At the end of that period, I finally became aware of myself and what steered me.

READY FOR CHANGE

I once said to myself, "I hate the way I look," when I looked in the mirror. Who am I kidding? It was every day. It was every time. I said the same message when someone was just looking at me too.

What a phrase to tell yourself all the time! I clearly wasn't happy with myself. There was a growing anxiety that made me feel uncomfortable. I remember talking to friends—people who I've known for years—and thinking, "Are they judging me?" or, "Am I saying something wrong?"

Why? I'm not sure. At least, I wasn't sure at the time. This internal dialogue affected my personal and professional lives, and you can imagine how many situations I avoided because of it.

Dating is an example. Not only are you supposed to meet one-on-one with people you barely know, but you're expected to share a piece of you intimately. How would I—someone who doesn't like me—think that another person would value anything that I told them about myself? It's an anxiety-producing situation worth avoiding—and I did that quite a bit.

For many years, I avoided ME. I avoided truly looking at myself until I reached this pinnacle of unhappiness—the bottom for me. I was sick of staring blankly at nothing while thinking about my life. I was sick of waking up every morning wondering what would go wrong today. I was sick of feeling alone in relationships. I was sick of being unhappy. On a wintry day in the back of a Starbucks on my 30th birthday, I was ready for change.

I started to piece the VERY complicated, imperfect puzzle of myself together and then embarked on my toughest journey: Looking at me.

I was searching for the next step in my life inside a coffee cup and a book called *The 4-Hour Workweek* by Timothy Ferriss. His book on how to minimize life's distraction and maximize efficiency in order to live more and work less wasn't the complete answer, but certainly a first step.

I wanted to create a strategy for the next tier of unknowns in my life. I wanted to be prepared to handle life efficiently! We'll call this obsessive, perfectionist ambition an excellent reflection of myself at the time.

Although I didn't entirely agree with Ferriss' thoughts about achieving wealth, the book had a significant impact on me. *The 4-Hour Workweek* encourages the reader to examine their fears and insecurities. I'd never taken this step. I examined myself in a whole new way and began to question my life and who I was:

- Am I truly happy with my job?
- Am I really listening to people around me?
- Why do I work as hard as I do?
- What do I fear?

These questions stabbed at my brain for days, leaving me stunned but intrigued. I was determined to give myself an honest critique of my life and plan the year ahead as an exploration into my unknown depths.

It took me awhile to face my inner self, but I began to realize the underpinnings of me—the negative and positive motivators that shaped my personal and professional lives. "Being aware" became a scary experience. At that point, my life was a time of flux and change. I was newly married, uncertain about the future of my personal training business, and trying to fix me, all while jumping into these unknowns. This task was more difficult than I had envisioned.

I began to unravel subconscious influences that had control over me. Part of me was an unrecognized butcher who snuck up behind my consciousness and cut off more than fat. He routinely carved off my self-esteem, my efforts, and who I was. This insecurity-driven persona trounced every "I can" statement and consistently judged what I looked like and how I did everything. He limited my ambition and altered my perspective of the world. He repeatedly reminded me that my life wasn't good enough—I wasn't good enough.

I recognized my ongoing internal battle and didn't know how to handle it. I also wasn't sure if other people were dealing with this, too. I was my worst enemy.

Eventually, I realized that I built the foundation of my business on the fear of failure. I was a square piece in a round marriage. I felt helpless. Somehow, I managed to make my life more complicated than before.

Then, I finally saw it and it was a significant first step. The secret to true happiness was already in my hands. I was always searching for ways outside of myself to reach this goal: Buying a new car, moving into a new home, and getting married. I never fully recognized the fears and insecurities that guided my behaviors, my perceived control, the lack of belief in myself, what influenced my decisions, and the effect of my environment on me.

I finally woke up. I finally became aware. I realized that the secret to happiness didn't involve just ADDING things to my life. It involved REMOVING them. Instead of always searching for an answer outside of me, I needed to look inside. The secret to redefining myself and achieving happiness was rewiring my MIND. I needed to remove the self-destructive, reinforced patterns and rewire my mind with new adaptive strategies. I needed to rewire the way I looked at myself.

I began creating a business plan for my life that gave me the confidence to interact with my environment in new ways and pursue what I wanted. My life was no longer about just wanting to fulfill the typical social goals of a successful job and family. It was about creating meaningful relationships, trusting myself, and working in a career congruent with my passions and purpose. It became about rewriting the definition of what happiness entails and how to achieve it.

My life became more efficient and less stressful with this new focus. I was gaining more in life with less effort. The only requirement: Staying aware!

This awareness was a return to the "simple" in my life. It was the breakdown of complicated scenarios, like my approach to marketing my business or how I handled a disagreement in my relationships.

My new mantra was, "keep it simple," and I did. With every new challenge, I was able to keep it simple and move closer to happiness and less self-doubt.

New pursuits became easier as I looked at them with a clearer vision. My fears and insecurities that plagued me for years no longer told me "don't do it." I replaced the message with, "I will find a way to do it."

You will too. I can give you the step-by-step process to achieve financial gain, weight loss, or anything else you want, but it won't work unless you remove the real obstacle: YOU.

Redefine Yourself will help you look at you for the first time. You will incorporate new adaptive strategies that will not only change your life, but positively impact those people around you. Truly redefining yourself will help you achieve the happiness you've always wanted.

Now is your time to REDEFINE YOU!

2

Practice Mindfulness

I BEGAN TO WONDER how many other things flew under my nose daily. What if I slowed life down? What would I see? I needed to become aware of the functional and dysfunctional world both around me and within me. I wanted to be a new person, but I needed to know what I was up against first. I needed to incorporate mindfulness into my life: a mental state achieved by focusing one's awareness on the present moment while calmly acknowledging and accepting one's feelings, thoughts, and bodily sensations.

A therapist might say, "let's start" by focusing on your breath. The monk, Bhante Henepola Gunaratana, once said: "When we truly observe the breath, we are automatically placed in the present." To achieve this state, you're not allowed to control your breath, and you must let your breath move in its natural rhythm (like while sleeping).

Lie back, relax, and focus on your breath moving in and out like waves massaging the shore. Any time there's a distraction—a thought about pressing projects at work, random characters on television shows you're watching, or anything else—place the idea on a boat and let the river take it away. Listen to every sound around you: A dog barking in the distance; the subtle cracks in the wood; your neighbors yelling at each other; your neighbors yelling at you for meditating on their front lawn; whatever it is, name it and continue to focus on your breath and...

Okay, I probably lost you. You either fell asleep or struggled to relax and focus on your breath. Your breathing might have become ragged because while you're trying not to control your breath, you feel an incessant need to force it. As you do this, it may cause you to begin breathing irregularly and move you away from a relaxed stress.

Meditation is initially stressful and the reason people avoid it. "It's so simple though," people will tell you. It's not. You've trained yourself to multitask and do a million things at once in everyday life. It's different to remove yourself from this mindset and slow down for a moment.

If you practice meditation, it will open your mind and help you look at your reality. Many people find that their reality is far more chaotic and disorganized than they ever imagined. You might have the same realization.

Unless you're the musician, Sting, who can meditate for four hours, any moment of mindfulness (awareness of now with total stimulation of your senses) is a success. With practice, you'll realize it isn't as hard as it seems—especially if it is only 10 seconds at a time. The goal is just to wake up to life around you—and inside of you—at any given moment. The toughest part is not passing judgment. You are just naming what you see, hear, smell, and think about. You are awakening yourself to a new reality.

In my phone, I found an application (Simple Routine) that allows me to schedule alerts throughout the day. I receive a "take a breath" alert four times and do this no matter where I am at or what I am doing. These reminders help me successfully integrate a form of meditation and mindfulness with minimal effort into my life.

When you practice mindfulness, you are returning to the simplest process of you: breathing. Start with a single breath. Breathe all of the way in; all of the way out. You want to inhale fully and then exhale. If a thought infiltrates this moment, name it and allow it to escape your mind peacefully. You can place your thoughts about work and other stresses onto a boat and push it a down 'that mental river'. You are slowing down your life for one moment. You are incorporating mindfulness into your life.

A few years ago, I first practiced meditation at the Mystical Yoga Farm on Lake Atitlan in Guatemala, just a few months after my divorce. Lake Atitlan stood in total solitude in the middle of three volcanoes. The sunrise peaked over the top of each volcano every morning and slowly lit the fog crawling over the water. It was the perfect setting for breathing and thinking about breathing.

It was also the setting for four days of alcohol-free socializing and vegetarian cooking. In between yoga and permaculture sessions, I snuck out to a hammock and wrote in my journal before falling asleep.

It was simplicity in its most natural form and freedom from the stresses of the world. It was a self-sustaining commune without the pressures from work, family, and everything else.

I pleasantly awoke every morning at 5 a.m. to the voice of a French woman singing outside of the cabins. It was a calm, gentle wake-up call—and a fitting one—before we embarked to the pier for morning meditation.

On the pier, the mix of guests from all over the world—German, Australian, South American, North American, and more—sat cross-legged and faced the sun hiding behind the volcanoes. Birds were chirping and flying toward the calm water, looking for food while a slowly rocking boat nearby made subtle sounds of wood rubbing on wood.

Now, picture me in the middle of this band of meditators, fidgeting and wondering why I am the only who can't cross his legs comfortably. I'm closing my eyes and listening to the subtle sounds of nature.

I begin to focus on the waves of breath with the guided help of our instructor.

And now...I wonder how the Chicago Bears football team played on Sunday...I wonder when we'll eat breakfast.

My left eye opens. I peer to my left and wonder, "Is anyone else distracted?" Then I close it before opening my right eye. "I mustn't be the only one." Funny enough, another American was doing the same.

I wasn't alone, but I felt like the first morning was a failure. The next few mornings I awoke early and practiced with my new American friend.

I improved and found what works for me: staring at moving water or the flame of a candle. In fact, by day four of my "mystical" journey, I stared at the candle for over three hours while seated in the same position.

I was able to focus on some "thing" moving while letting my breath flow naturally. I found a way to jump outside of my thoughts and separate myself from them: the routine of life, the pull of my business, or any other stressors.

I still practice this in small amounts in my daily life. The best example of this takes place during disagreements with my girlfriend. I have a tendency to overreact and raise my voice. And in these metacognition moments, I remove myself from ME and focus on my breath. I concentrate on full inhalation and exhalation. It's during these moments that I have now been able to take a breath, concentrate on the now, and remove myself from instinct and emotion – and I don't need to meditate for hours to do this. I'm able to slow my thinking and regain control over a moment. I sometimes catch myself thinking, "Why am I overreacting?" or "Why am I saying this?" while it's happening. I recognize the irrational words before I begin to speak them.

I've been able to do this after work now, too. Here is a recent journal entry to illustrate the point:

I'm lying on the couch looking out the open patio door at the illuminated Chicago night sky, sucking in breaths of brisk March air. The bourbon rolling over the contours of my tongue is a relaxing retreat from a steady 13-hour day of mental and physical movement.

Each burning sip is a momentous reminder of now. A long awaited-second to feel the air around me again and taste every drop on my tongue.

Flashes of tomorrow's reality fly through my mind like a thunderous freight train shaking my very membrane of relaxation. Little by little, the sound disappears, and the train becomes distant as the subtle sounds of a passing car float above my balcony.

It's wonderful to hear those noises again.

These are the moments I cherish the most, and I hope you can find them too at the end of your day. Work is a given in life—our biggest obligation—but it doesn't have to control every part of our clock. You should never forget the peace of lying in place and letting that train pass. You should never forget to breathe. This journal entry is a reminder for me. I cherish that moment and often think about it when I'm knee-deep in craziness.

Focusing on your breath takes practice, and you should practice mindfulness in less stressful situations, too.

When I returned from Guatemala, I was excited to explore the world I already knew: Chicago. I couldn't help but wonder what I had been missing up to this point. I decided to head to one of the most popular shopping areas in Chicago: Michigan Avenue. On that Saturday afternoon, it was an active street of shopping tourists. When I arrived, I stood on the sidewalk in front of the department store Nieman Marcus motionless while droves of people passed me in every direction.

Subtle insults flew by my ears while I looked up, down, and around me. Clearly, people weren't happy that I stopped in the middle of a moving crowd and obstructed their path to shopping. I wanted to halt the flow of traffic in my life to take a moment.

Very few times had I ever stopped, looked, and listened to everything around me. I was so wrapped up in my business, fantasy football, and many other insignificant things in my life at home that I never truly allowed myself to take in every sound, sight, smell, and breath of air.

For the first time, I looked down the block and saw several homeless people huddled in random alleys while shoppers walked by with their shopping bags, completely unaware.

A man was in tattered clothes at the corner of the Wrigley Building talking to himself—why was this not abnormal for people? A person was living on the street and talking to himself. Society wouldn't dictate this behavior as normal, yet it was nothing extraordinary or worthy of attention for the passing shoppers.

I found out that this was more common than I thought, and I was surrounded by it daily. I can't say that this was the realization that I was looking for on that day. It did remind me of what I was overlooking, however. While mindfulness will open your world of awareness, it will also show you the good, the bad, and the ugly. You'll need to accept what you find for the time being before creating the life you want.

Today, you'll start by taking a breath.

REFLECTION SECTION

1. Awareness: Describe the streams of thought that pass through your mind while you focus on your breath.

2. Acceptance: How will you bypass these thoughts and focus on your breath again? What mental images will you help return to your relaxed state?

3. Adaptation: What stressful moments in your life will benefit from this form of meditation? When and how will you practice meditation?

3

Listen to Your Inner Voice

AWARENESS EXTENDS BEYOND SIMPLE identification of the world. You must also listen to the inner voice that guides you. In order to do this, you must become an outside observer to the mechanics of your mind and think about your thinking.

Psychologists have termed this process of cognitive thinking metacognition. Metacognition is "you" understanding the thought process behind your decision to grab a cupcake even though you're trying to lose weight. It is "you" catching yourself making negative statements about you while randomly doing other things.

When I started to think about thinking, I began analyzing every nook and cranny of my brain, questioning its existence and intent. Why did I continue to place myself in the same self-destructive situation over and again?

It was like clockwork. I'd push my projects at work back until the very last minute, and then the perfectionist in me would place stress on myself to complete it right and on time. Meanwhile, my subconscious was telling me that "the project could still be a little better", or, "you'll never finish this by the deadline."

The stress was always overwhelming, and it affected the way I treated others. At times, I avoided conversations or kept them to a minimum.

I realized that I needed to go deeper into ME to gain a better understanding. Once I did, I found that an unconscious voice narrated my actions and thoughts. This voice provided the mental script for my daily life. You will discover the same in yourself.

This unconscious voice—my self-talk—was the narrator in my mind that told me what to do and how to perceive things. It was a James Earl Jones-like voice that directed me based on past experiences, traumas, insecurities, fears, and outside images.

Because it dictates the trends, patterns, and little idiosyncrasies that make up your world, this is more than enough reason to begin thinking about thinking. Who knows what the James Earl Jones voice is telling you every day? You don't want to replace the guy; you just want him to read a new script. You have followed the same one for quite some time; now is the time to rewrite it. Redefining yourself means rewriting your mental script to achieve happiness.

I'll never forget the story my friend Tim shared about the first time he recognized his inner voice.

It was a weekend void of work—and much else for that matter—and Tim jumped in the shower, a seemingly benign and routine activity. The shower was also a time for the idle mind run wild, and this particular day was no different, when the following thought popped into his head unprompted: "I hate my life."

Tim was worried. Why would he tell himself this? His job and personal life had been great. Was there an insecurity or fear that led to this message? Did someone say it to him? How often did he subconsciously repeat this statement? Did it change the way he interacted with people or participated in life?

A negative message like this tends to stem from insecurities and fears. You too may have developed them as a child or when bombarded with the wrong messages from work-driven, high-pressured teachers, parents or employers. Your inner voice can be very convincing and destructive. It can also hold you back from a goal or rip your self-esteem to shreds.

How does this happen? Tim probably wasn't filtering the development of these messages throughout his daily life. His mind is a talking parrot repeating whatever was said or seen, building stronger and stronger associations with the world inside and outside of him. Whatever the message, it was probably reinforced or in the process of being reinforced through repeated exposure. It is an example of the messages that our minds learn intentionally and unintentionally.

Pay attention to the messages that you tell yourself. When you practice meditation, mindfulness, and slowing down for a moment to become more aware, this voice is far louder than you ever realized. What does it say? It may have a far more negative influence on how you feel or what you do than you imagine. There's no doubt that the "I can't do it" messages that I told myself for years held me back from taking chances in my business or being more intimate in my romantic relationships.

Don't be mistaken; having an inner voice is a strength as much as it is a weakness. We can be very convincing to ourselves, and this is especially important when we need reassurance or confidence. It will often be your inner coach giving you a constant pep talk to "take a leap of faith", or, give you advice or perspective when you need it most.

Your new goal is to wake up to life around you—and inside of you—at any given moment. It is during these times that you will be able to take a moment, breathe, focus on the now, and remove yourself from instinct and emotion.

Typically, people begin this transformation process by observing their inner voice, behaviors, and environment. They follow this step with an analysis of their trends and patterns, also known as figuring out 'why you do what you do.' You can try to discover the origin of any negative message. You don't want similar messages from the same source, and you certainly don't want them reinforced.

It is an intriguing process, but it can also be a scary one. You may open a box of feelings from your childhood that has consequently affected your decision to do something over 20, 30, or 40 years later. It can be a strange, weird, sad, or intriguing experience.

You may start placing blame on others or yourself. You may ask yourself, "Am I a good person?", or, "Am I screwed up?" It could result in a tailspin of fears and insecurities.

It's very easy to judge—especially yourself. It takes effort and practice to look at you objectively. Just like other unconscious truths about you, you must decide how deep you wish to go and how much time you spend on each message.

Either way, you'll need to replace negative messages with positive messages. You may also need to provide proof for yourself that these messages aren't real.

I am a visual person: I need to see the messages in front of me. If I tell myself "I'm not a good personal trainer," I look for evidence to dispute this claim. I read positive reviews from clients who enjoyed their personal training experiences with me. This strategy may work for you too. The following positive messages may help you overcome your fears, insecurities, irrational emotional reactions, and more:

- I can overcome this.
- My history proves the inaccuracy of this negative message.
- I will only think rationally about this situation.
- I will always try to be my best self despite my imperfections.
- I am prepared to handle any unknown.
- I can change this situation even though I can't do it right now.

- I love who I am and accept the little idiosyncrasies of my being.
- Fears and insecurities disappear as quickly as they appear.
- I will be strong enough to face my fear again.
- My insecurities are irrational.
- I have the power to redefine myself.
- I have the control to change my environment.
- I have the control over my happiness at work.

With the right practice, you will develop the power to reinforce a strong message—a message that can drive you to new heights and triumph over your weaknesses.

REFLECTION SECTION

1. Awareness: Listen to you inner voice for the next day and then describe three negative messages that you notice. What triggered each of these messages?

How often does your inner voice repeat these messages? How do you think they affect your behavior or how you feel about yourself?

2. Acceptance: Are you willing to accept that it may take time to change these messages?

3. Adaptation: How will you change these messages? What evidence can you find to disapprove the messages? What positive messages can you tell yourself instead?

4

·····························

Face Your Fears

FEAR IS A VERY powerful influence, and you should question how it affects your decisions and approaches. How many times have you avoided a situation because of fear? Have you ever backed out of a presentation at work? Have you ever taken a different path to avoid an abrasive person?

Although the fear can lead your to avoidance, is it always a bad thing? No. Fear can protect you from potentially harmful situations. The mind automatically triggers its efficient response system when it recognizes a learned threat. This system of fear has grown inside of you based on past experiences or what you've learned.

If an experience or something else has built a strong enough association, the mind will make it tough to forget and will consequently hide it in our subconscious like a protective mechanism. It usually takes repeated experiences before you internally say to yourself, "Maybe I shouldn't drive erratically because I will hit another car," or, "Maybe I shouldn't work 10 hours per day in a stressful job because I'm at risk for a heart attack." Either way, it can help you avoid destructive or stressful situations. This inner voice is quite essential when we need a wake-up call from life's distractions.

We need to remember that our minds thrive on reinforcement and don't always effectively decipher between good and bad or rational and irrational. The fear of flying is a common example, and one which I can relate to.

Rocking back and forth by the open door of the plane, I looked down 13,000 feet on a still landscape of cornfields and a distant Lake Michigan. Three seconds later my tandem partner pushed me out, and we free-fell 5,000 feet before my parachute popped open. That was the first and only time I ever skydived.

Funny enough, I wasn't scared while crouching on the edge of the doorway. The experience was surreal; however, I didn't feel that way 30 seconds earlier.

Most people have a fear of heights, and I can't blame them. The higher we travel, the less likely we'll survive in the case of an accident. This fear is a survival instinct.

On that day, though, the height didn't scare me (or the fear of dropping 13,000 feet with a parachute, which is safe, but still crazy). Above all, the plane ride scared me the most.

The plane was a ten-person, single-engine plane. As it rose up into the sky, you heard the engine roar through the cabin as the wind knocked the plane back and forth like a pinball. I looked down at my new altimeter wristwatch and saw the steady climb in elevation. I had never been more nervous in my life. At the same time, I couldn't wait to jump.

Why was I more scared of the plane than the actual jump? If you think about it, being in a closed cabin seems safer and more controlled than a free-fall with plastic strapped to your back.

That thought never crossed my mind, though. I couldn't stop thinking about all the small planes I had seen on the news, including the plane carrying JFK Jr. that had crashed and killed everyone on board. I had a constant newsreel showing me these horrible images and bylines of those fatal crashes playing in my head.

My fear is an excellent tool for survival—when it's rational. I finally understood why many people fear flying. Despite this fear, though, I still flew up and jumped after debating whether or not I should. I finally realized that it wasn't rational to fear flying on that day. The weather conditions were sunny and warm, and the airline had a perfect flight history. It's hard to believe that fear almost steered me from an unbelievable experience.

It truly is a problem when irrational fears overtake our being. Despite our efforts at times to repress or erase them, they tend to scratch and claw their way out like a cat trapped in a bag. They pop up in our minds as thoughtful, rational monologues that appear in our best interests, but are actually self-sabotaging pushes to maintain our current culture, like a familiar job or relationship, even though it causes us stress.

It doesn't seem to make sense. Why would we allow these things to ruminate within us? Why would we allow them to take over our being when we're not paying attention?

For you, it may manifest itself in an underlying voice telling you "Don't do this!" Despite your best efforts to eliminate the message, it continues to torment you as an unfiltered guided voice; much like it did to me as I was preparing to board that small plane.

We carve our experiences and our interactions into a writeable disc that plays the background music to our life. Unfortunately—and fortunately—fears are written on the disc along the way, too. They make a deeper groove, and it takes more repetitions to change them.

You need to face your fears by defining their influence on your perspective and behavior, and by repeatedly reinforcing a positive message. Don't feel the pressure to figure out the root of every fear. It may take more work than you're willing to handle.

It's time to redefine the legacy of fear within you.

REFLECTION SECTION

1. Awareness: Name three fears that steer your behavior (e.g., avoidance, projection, isolation, etc.). Where have these fears stemmed from and what evidence do you have to justify listening to these fears?

2. Acceptance: Are you prepared to face these fears again with a new self-confidence? If not, what positive message can you repeatedly reinforce? How will you carry this out?

3. Adaptation: Which fears are unjustified and how will you no longer allow them to change your approach? What positive messages can you reinforce repeatedly to convince yourself that these fears aren't rational?

5

Extinguish Your Insecurities

INSECURITIES CAN POSSESS AN element of truth (I say this cautiously). Nevertheless, they are primarily based on YOUR perspective and how YOU think or know people respond to the issue at hand (e.g., weight, hair, athletic ability, dancing skills, etc.).

Insecurities embody the root of the word—they are something that makes you feel less secure. Physical safety isn't usually the problem. Most likely, your ego and emotional security are threatened instead.

How many times a day does insecurity steer you? Wouldn't it be easier if you weren't worried about how you look or do something? Does it consume you? Does it really matter?

Most likely it does not matter. I would love to tell you to accept what you can't change at the moment, sweep what other people think under the rug and move on to shaping the happiest, most purposeful life you can. We all know it isn't this easy, although it IS part of the answer.

Like fears, our insecurities are ingrained from repeated reinforcement over the years or are traumatic scars, and you can't just push them off a cliff.

I hated my height in grade school. I felt abnormal, like a giant. I slouched at my desk to make sure I wasn't any different from anyone else.

However, I don't believe anyone ever ridiculed me for being tall. I just felt different from everyone else, and it was a feeling I had quite often. You would have thought that I would've been more insecure about the dorky, thick, gray-rimmed glasses I was wearing. Thank you to the 1980s for acceptance!

I now realize the ridiculousness of those thoughts when I reflect on that period of my life. As an adult, my height is often valued and complemented. I walk into a room, and my height virtually announces my presence. It is an asset in many professional settings as well as when changing the batteries in fire alarms.

I didn't believe it was an asset when I was a kid, though, and I changed my behavior and how I interacted with others because of this.

Although we can't eliminate our insecurities, Aristotle taught that they need to be leashed and managed. Heck, anything that steers our behavior requires restraint. We are trying to drive our behavior and perspective for our best selves. We shouldn't allow irrational thoughts to misguide us.

Until recently, they certainly misguided me. Before my divorce, I remember lying in my darkened bedroom with only the repetitive sound of a box fan on a sleepless night. It was 4 a.m., and I had been staring at the ceiling for the last four hours. My wife at the time was still at work (overnight police officer), and I laid there with pinball thoughts streaming through my head, occasionally bumping the inner shell of my skull. A nervous rush of energy flowed to my throat causing a wide eyed look of little sleep. I only slept two hours that night.

That was the fourth day in a row, and I couldn't escape the prison of my mind. The mental tumble in my mind placed my body on constant alert (without sleep) and within a state of repetitious introspection. The darting thoughts continually infiltrated my physical existence despite my efforts to push it from my mind.

My anxiety was at its worse, and I felt like I was drowning. Uncertainty was overcoming me. Why was I in this relationship? What was I doing with my career? Why was I always unhappy?

In the real sense of my perfectionist self, I began researching my mind. I tried to understand the mistakes and everything else that continued to pierce it. My new, relentless dedication sent me further into my hole. The new understanding of me led to a constant state of wonder and confusion. It was difficult to think objectively about myself. I tied my emotion to every thought process, and it was tough to separate the two.

Thoughts of insecurity still took over: "you're not good enough," "settle," "it is your fault," etc. These messages were examples of the constant subconscious struggle that plagued me ever since grade school. I realized my lack of confidence and how I persistently pushed all the boundaries in order to achieve perfection. My subconscious self always whispered in my ear "that isn't good enough, keep pushing."

I wanted to change my mindset at that very moment but couldn't. Why, even with my best efforts, could I not overturn this thought process? Why did my processing of the world and myself continue to shake my confidence and self-control? The questions remained unanswered, and my mindset revealed underlying insecurities that I wasn't aware of—insecurities that were beyond my consciousness. The anxiety and unhappiness I felt was more than a surface disagreement. It was a battle with my insecurities: my lack of confidence around beautiful women, my parents, or bosses; my uncertainty of who I was and what I felt; and the fear that what I did wasn't good enough.

On that night, I finally realized that I allowed my insecurities to overrun my life. For over twenty years, I repeatedly reinforced negative thoughts about myself until they became ingrained.

Without a doubt, it was important to identify these insecurities. I needed to face them. I listed them on paper and asked myself, "Is there evidence to believe that this is true?" If they were true, I wondered how I could modify them. If I couldn't change them, though, I knew I had to accept them and disregard other people's reactions to them.

I began redefining myself by reinforcing a more positive perspective. Every time I heard a negative thought I responded with a positive mental yell: "Insecurities disappear as quickly as they appear!" When an insecurity steered my path, I told myself, "I define my life by the happiness I bring to my family and friends!" I began scheduling positive alerts on my phone to pop up randomly throughout the day, and I read them over and over and over.

You should challenge an emotional root that has planted itself in your unconscious through strong reinforcement. While it seems like I've just oversimplified a complicated mental process, the first solution is always returning to the simplest state.

In your efforts, you need to rationalize a new message positively and repeatedly in order to combat that evil inner message. You did it when facing your fears, and now you'll do it to extinguish your insecurities. It can be tiresome and often force you to question whether or not you're strong enough to handle it. The toughest part is not allowing yourself to get in the way, and you must continuously tell yourself positive messages daily. It is the art of repetition, and it works just as much mentally as it does physically for a sport.

As you examine the root of your insecurities, you must determine the depth of investigation. You may need outside sources to remind you-your phone, your friends, your family, your religious leader, or a professional like a life coach or therapist, who can be an unbiased mental arbitrator.

No matter what, though, the process for mental and emotional recovery is the same, and it requires a purposeful change in mindset with proper rationalization and repetition.

REFLECTION SECTION

1. Awareness: Name three insecurities that steer your behavior (e.g., weight, hair, athletic ability, dancing skills, etc.). Where have these insecurities stemmed from and what evidence do you have to justify listening to these insecurities?

2. Acceptance: Are you prepared to face these insecurities again with a new self-confidence? If not, what positive message can you repeatedly reinforce? How will you carry this out?

3. Adaptation: How will you no longer allow these insecurities to change your perspective and approach? What positive messages can you reinforce repeatedly to convince yourself that these insecurities aren't rational?

6

Practice Emotional Restraint

FORTUNATELY AND UNFORTUNATELY, OUR emotions are so powerful that we can't ignore them. After all, they affect our interpretation of the world and our interaction with it. They also steer our decision-making processes and how we approach a problem.

Most important, emotions bind a thought to our mind and give it value. Your emotion heightens your love for your kids and pushes you to create positive change in the world. It enhances an experience and gives you character. Your emotional output is part of your identity.

It isn't great, though, when you're upset with your spouse, and you violently throw something across the living room. It probably isn't the best when anger overcomes you so much that you're bitter towards anyone you see afterward.

I think about the little moments in my life where I went "just a little too far" without emotional restraint. I'm not sure how many times I've pushed and pushed even though I needed to walk away. There were countless arguments that could've ended sooner if I would've just stepped away or quieted my mind. Instead, I spewed senseless material from the usual internal script.

Even when I was right (in my opinion, of course), I lost credibility because of my childish emotional outpour. I always resorted to my Neanderthal approach to disagreements. Like the Incredible Hulk, I found my blood pressure boiling slowly while discussing a heated topic. It's almost as if I couldn't wait to share my point of view—instead of listening, I would usually cut my girlfriend off so that I didn't forget my ever-so-important point.

I became anxious and uneasy. My words would always fall helplessly from my mouth. Often I thought, "Why am I saying this?", as I said it. Such heightened emotional states usually steered me from the foundation of the disagreement and led to bitterness between my partner and me.

This type of emotional outpour not only changes the dynamic of any conversation, but the wake of emotions may consequently impact other non-participating victims in its path. It takes you further away from rationality and efficiently handling any problem or disagreement.

On the other hand, passion provides the horsepower and drive for any pursuit. Like any wild animal, though, it can prove to be uncontrollable if not tamed or properly guided with reinforcement.

Aristotle suggests to "cultivate virtue by learning how to manage one's passions." Management is a necessity for anything that is a force, like our internal emotional, wild animal. Like all machines, power without restraint or management can steer you in less than desirable directions. Consequently, your emotional behavior may lead you further from the development, adaptation, and carry-through of a virtuous and happy life.

What does this mean for you? Redefining yourself means developing a cool head that will allow you to see the whole picture without a filter. It requires you to become aware of your reactions and the underlying causes. Is there positive intent? Does it stem from a fear or insecurity?

At the end of the day, though, your reaction is based on your emotional interpretation of the situation, and this could play out differently depending on your environment and your level of self-awareness.

When it comes to relationships now, I've held Aristotle's idea close to my heart as a reminder of the necessity of managing my emotions. I employ metacognition and realize why I stress easily and what triggers my reactions. More times than not in these situations, I feel irrationally defensive, or I fear losing my thought.

As I change this reaction, I recognize how my partner feels, and I listen to her WHOLE point. I've also realized that it's good to step away when needed, especially if I'm overwhelmed with emotion. This applies to both my personal and professional lives. I'm not entirely avoiding the issue, but instead just allowing my frontal lobe to decrease its 'emotional temperature.'

It took many experiences to have this realization, and I consistently practice reinforcing this new habit. Quite frankly, I witness many people struggle with the same thing—the challenge of separating emotion from reason in everyday life when facing a problem. While under the constant stress and the endless demands of life, outcomes are less controlled and can consequently result in an emotional spew.

We know that our passions steer us towards rewarding pursuits, like higher education or better parenting. Clearly, though, our passion can get in the way of fully understanding our environment and ourselves, too (as well as your partner's side of the story).

We want to embrace emotion but also understand how it influences our path and interpretation of the world, and also be able to leash it when needed. Most important, we need to recognize what can drive our emotions and the coping behaviors that result.

REFLECTION SECTION

1. Awareness: Describe three scenarios in which your emotional reaction steered you from rational behavior (e.g., a disagreement with your spouse, reprimanding your child, confronting your boss, etc.). Where do these emotions stem from and what evidence do you have to justify reacting in that manner?

2. Acceptance: Will you accept that your emotional restraint could have improved past scenarios? If not, do you believe that you could have handled the situations slightly different to reduce the stress of the scenario?

3. Adaptation: How will you practice emotional restraint when confronted with stressful scenarios next time? Describe three specific strategies based on the scenarios above. If developing a plan is difficult at this time, refer to Chapter 13: Approach New Problems With Confidence for help.

7

Believe That You Can Redefine Yourself

BELIEF IS THE SEED for change. What you say to yourself repeatedly will help you reach this state of confidence. By practicing positive self-talk, you are convincing yourself that you can overcome, achieve, and persevere. You want to reach the point in which you genuinely believe that you can redefine yourself. Otherwise, you will constantly be battling the inner evil self that will continue to keep you in a state of unhappiness.

I don't encourage 'blind belief'—an ego-driven, pseudo-attitude that is only as strong as the fears and insecurities that it is built on. Don't allow your personality to put on a show of confidence. Draw the curtains and end the show.

It's time to face yourself and not worry about what other people think. Convince yourself that real change requires a change in mindset and believe that you can do it.

When it comes to this changing of your mindset, nothing seems to be tougher than quitting smoking. John, one of my long-time clients and greatest friends, loved smoking. Early in his career, John spent every night surrounded by cigarettes—welcome to the life of a bartender and bar owner. The smell and sight of smoke was a satisfying sensory cloud to help bring calm to the stress of the night. For John, it was release from an industry based on drinking and constant movement.

Let's break down the reality of cigarette smoking: it yellows your teeth and fingers and makes your hair smell like an ashtray. They increase your blood pressure, decrease your lung capacity, and cause elevated levels of stress. You would think that all this would be enough to deter people from smoking and make them stop. It doesn't.

I can see why. James Dean still looks cool while smoking in his movies. We may also have a secret affinity towards fire and smoke; after all, I was transfixed by the light of a simple candle while meditating in Guatemala.

Interestingly, people continue with the habit despite their ambitious health goals. Nearly 20% of my clients smoke cigarettes, many of whom don't realize I know. Meanwhile, many others confess to me as if I'm the priest of health. They want a healthy lifestyle, but they never kick the habit. They'll do everything in their power to give up everything else except for the one thing they need to. I've seen one month, six month, and two-year attempts that have culminated in the eventual return to the one thing they want the most.

Eventually, John wanted to quit for health reasons. Although he began taking the prescription drug Chantix to help him quit, he failed.

Within two years of this attempt, though, John successfully quit smoking. He believed that change was feasible and tried using Chantix again. Although the habit of smoking was a chemical dependence, it still took more than taking a prescription drug to quit. It took confidence and constant reminders (self-talk) to overcome his want (the perceived need). With medication and a concentration on being mindful, John revealed the key to change. He believed he could do it, and eventually he did. Even though it was tough, he kept telling himself that same message: "I want to quit."

Like John, I didn't believe that I possessed the power to change. Instead of building a life of fulfillment, I shifted my efforts towards an illusion of happiness. Self-doubt was my nemesis, and it controlled my being. Although I often recognized my unhappiness, I never believed that I can change it.

Nothing was sweeter than the Starbucks moment I previously described. It was an initial spark of hope that I could, in fact, live a happy life and a belief that life didn't have to be what it was.

It's time to light the same fire inside of you.

REFLECTION SECTION

1. Awareness: Describe three goals that you failed to achieve over
    the last year. Why do you believe you failed to reach those goals
    and what evidence do you have to support these claims?

2. Acceptance: Are you prepared to accept that you failed to reach these goals once before? What obstacles would you face if you pursued these goals again?

3. Adaptation: What new strategies can you possibly utilize to overcome these barriers and achieve your goals? How can you modify these goals to make them attainable? What messages can you tell yourself to remain positive and focused on your goals?

8

Regain Control Over Your Life

DO YOU EVER FEEL completely powerless?

Although I did before that day in Starbucks, I now realize that there is always something I can do, that I have control, and can always do something about any situation I face. While I didn't know what was in store for me at the time, I had the power to be my best self within my strengths and limitations and make the most of my experiences. Feeling a sense of self-control isn't defined as 'controlling every unknown.' Instead, it's defined as 'feeling confident about your approach, accepting the consequences, and adapting whenever and wherever needed.'

If you feel helpless, it is difficult to achieve the self-control you desire. You developed the perspective that no matter what you do, it won't change the outcome. Time after time, your efforts have been fruitless. What's the point of trying to change anything now? You are a forever pessimist, and you can always give reasons why life isn't great.

Feeling a lack of control over your life can be stressful. It reminds me of a sailboat careening out of control during a hurricane. Even if the captain possesses the expertise to meander through most storms, she doesn't have the tools to handle this particular storm. The crew will do whatever they can while water swallows each side and the boat rocks violently back and forth.

Their efforts seem like perfect reactions to each new wind and wave but are never enough to combat the flooding waters on the ship. What else can they do? Their ship is slowly sinking, and the crew feels powerless despite doing everything they can to save it.

Many people can relate to this story of survival. You and your significant other work six days a week but never seem to recover financially—there's always another car part required or the kids needing something for school.

You seek a moment of peace at work, but there's always an unfinished project or a complaint from a customer or colleague that you're dealing with. Day in and day out, you're trying to climb to even ground, but your efforts are never enough. You feel powerless. Clients have shared similar situations with a look of frustration, fatigue, and burnout.

Your story may be different but also feel the same. Financial burden or an unfulfilling job plagues you. Your relationship is spiraling out of control. You deal with significant stresses, and you don't know how to change them.

If you were telling me your story like many of my clients have before (sometimes through tears), you would probably say there's nothing you can do about it. "It is what it is," or "You don't understand," are typical answers. You might downplay your ability to make a change or affirm that you are powerless.

That feeling of powerlessness can show itself in many ways. In an effort to limit that feeling and minimize the unknowns in my life, I once lived a structured, rigid life defined by rigorous routine, constant introspection, and the daily analysis of every moment. My life was hardly enjoyable. Any wrinkle that appeared in my life became a pure disruption to my obsessed and meticulously-planned out life. Premeditated strategies steered my life. There was little room for the unknown.

Interestingly, a strict routine with constant achievements never made me feel secure, however. I was always achieving feats of success and pushing for more of them, while rarely enjoying the small moments. My college experience substantially demonstrated this. My resume was a summary of defining attributes that would supposedly help me obtain the perfect job, but it was never good enough. I couldn't escape feeling like I was completely powerless over my future.

Let's say that maybe up to this point you were right about similar situations. You joined a master's degree program with the hope of stable employment, but still bounce from job to job unhappily. You committed to marriage counseling for a year, but you still can't resolve the marital issues.

Maybe you were wrong. Maybe you didn't try everything you could because you didn't think of the solution, or you weren't in the right time and place for it to happen. Maybe it wasn't in your power to change your relationship, but it was in your power to build a new one with the right pieces.

You see, you're always in control but just haven't defined it in the right way. The world is full of too many unknowns, and it isn't plausible to think you can control all of it. It would be an endless effort.

However, you CAN control your perspective and approach. In fact, you have COMPLETE ownership, and nobody can take that away from you.

If one way fails, you can choose another way (or at least attempt it). Choice is your power, and you are not as leashed to a situation as you think you might be. If something can be changed or switched, I recommend trying it. Experiment. What do you have to lose?

If you can't change your situation, at least you modify something else for now—your perspective. You can reweave your mind with the pieces in front of you. Realign your perspective with your purpose—what you feel you were meant to do (a conversation we'll discuss in-depth later on). Flip your perspective of the negative into the positive.

Let's be honest. Your negativity has most likely placed a filter on your perspective of everything in front of you. It has held you back from stepping forward.

You are most likely overlooking the positives and small pieces for a path to redefine yourself. Think about your life as a game of Tetris: if you spin the object or flip it over, it will eventually fit perfectly into another piece of your life. If it doesn't, toss it aside and choose another piece.

"But Michael, I hear crazy Russian music and the game is too fast. I don't have time to flip the pieces constantly."

Perhaps you're right. You may need to slow the game down. Are you willing to do this? Are you prepared to make a sacrifice to achieve your best and happiest self?

An optimistic attitude is what you need. It is a belief that you have control and can create change. If you can't change your job right now, you will accept that and begin learning how you can operate in that position more happily. If you can't change your relationship right now, you will accept that and begin looking for ways to become a more effective partner in that partnership.

You can indeed wait forever for change to happen organically beyond your control. However, if you want it immediately, change will only occur if you BELIEVE that you have control over your situation and the environment. How about that? It's empowering to know that you have the power to steer away from stress or unhappiness! Just believe it.

REFLECTION SECTION

1. Awareness: Describe three scenarios in your personal life in which you feel helpless. Where does this feeling of helplessness stem from and what evidence do you have to support this lack of control?

2. Acceptance: Are you willing to accept that your life isn't perfect right now, but that you have the power to modify the situation or otherwise change your perspective?

3. Adaptation: What new strategies can you possibly utilize to take control over these scenarios? Is there a way to modify your perspective to feel a sense of control? If so, how? What messages can you tell yourself to remain positive?

9

Find Control Over Your Happiness at Work

PEOPLE INHERENTLY WANT TO contribute to something greater—not just quarterly goals. You want to know that your efforts in the office will help the company grow and create innovative products. You want to know that you are a piece of something bigger—an idea. You're unhappy, and you feel like a pawn on someone else's board, with no feeling of satisfaction in your daily role.

If this is true, are you ready to adapt however and wherever needed and accept the consequences? Are you prepared to take control over your happiness at work?

Take the time to consider your role. You're subject to the quarterly goals and billable hours that your managers demand of you. You feel the need to meet their bottom line, otherwise your job is in jeopardy.

Eventually, your passion for the content and type of your work disappears. You feel disassociated with your professional life. Before you know it, this unhappiness and lack of fulfillment carries over to your personal life. You react to loved ones with anger or isolation while dealing with work pressures. You dread the repetition of an unchangeable life each morning.

Can you release your emotional investment in this job for happiness elsewhere? Will you sacrifice many years of law school or graduate school and loans for a more gratifying job or position? Will you accept a job that pays less? Will you sacrifice possessions for pure happiness?

Most of you will say no and stay in your current job. Is this driven by the fears or insecurities that we discussed earlier? Possibly. But you may have other reasons: you don't want to sacrifice your income for possessions that you love, or you must take care of your family.

Have you ever looked at other options? Have you ever stepped out of your boundaries and pursued something out of the familiar? Have you ever taken a chance?

Let's accept that finding a new job or starting a new career is difficult. Can you find new satisfaction with the work instead? If you are a manager, you may be able to restructure your department to create a more positive and fulfilling atmosphere. In fact, you may have the power to redefine your position in a way that keeps you productive while keeping you in line with the responsibilities you enjoy the most.

If you're not a manager, you probably can't change the company structure around you—only yourself. The first step is realizing this and reexamining your current position. You may realize that the traditional business culture and mindset is the cause of your unhappiness.

For example, your managers may be steering you away from creative or extraordinary thinking, enticing you with bonuses and other carrot-and-stick rewards in order to meet the bottom line goals. As a result, you lose focus on the "now" while trying to meet the demands of someone else. You also lose focus on your own needs while you fulfill your manager's requirements. It's a pattern of living that you might accept despite your unhappiness.

It's not your fault. Our education system is partly responsible for these patterns. Teachers valued end results over effort and creativity. They constantly pushed you toward a particular goal without the opportunity for individuality and ownership. Your teachers encouraged "standardized thinking": a single/non-creative thought process fostered and structured by someone else.

If you can't leave your job, how will you change this? How will you take control over your position and reshape it in a way that brings fulfillment to you? Should you reevaluate your role in the company? Is it time to change or redefine your position so that it fosters autonomy? Is it time to request a position that values your creativity and judgment? At what point do you take responsibility for your contributions to work?

I followed this advice for several years while dancing through jobs as a restaurant server, cook, and teacher. Redefining your job status isn't easy. I was constantly redefining my position in someone else's company, and I never felt fulfilled. I was meeting someone else's quota and knew I could've done more in that position. Ironically, when I asked to "do more", managers always encouraged me to step back. They wanted to maintain the "status quo."

I aggressively pursued careers related to my degrees (psychology, sociology, and social science secondary education), but I felt like something was missing. I shook up the pieces of my life again and finally found the combination that worked for me at the age of 26 (while most of my friends started their careers around 21/22). I was eager and ambitious to find and shape the best life for me. I could've settled for the positions related to my degrees, but I didn't. I wanted something better and wouldn't give up fighting for it.

I began a business during my last three months of waiting tables and substitute teaching. By the end of that period, my personal training business was my only focus. Over nine years later, I still own my business and feel fortunate to have had the UNBELIEVABLE support of my clients. They gave me the option to have the perfect job for me, and I'm forever indebted.

Although my job wouldn't exist without their support, I couldn't have done this unless I BELIEVED I could do it and made the decision to take control over my situation and make it happen.

I'm not asking you to quit your job and start a business. It isn't for everyone. I'm asking you to take the pieces in your hand (life) and shake them up. If you fail in your first pursuit, shake again and again and again until you find your it. I want you to want something better, and never give up fighting for it. Take control over your career now and shape your position into a fulfilling one.

REFLECTION SECTION

1. Awareness: Do you feel a sense of fulfillment in your profes-
    sional role? What contributes to this feeling and do you believe
    that you have the control to change it? Why or why not?

2. Acceptance: Are you willing to accept that your professional life isn't perfect right now, but that you have the power to modify the situation or change your perspective?

3. Adaptation: What new strategies can you possibly utilize to take control over your professional life? How can you shape a fulfilling professional position?

10

Change the Way You Decide

ALTHOUGH YOU DON'T REALIZE it, your gut instincts and rationality influence your large and small decisions daily. It's important to examine how your decision-making process affects you. You may be causing yourself more stress than you know by not trusting your gut or overanalyzing these decisions.

During your search for a perfect option, decisions—like buying a house or choosing a career—may require never-ending research. At the end of the day, though, some decisions just rely on a hunch or a gut instinct.

Our experiences, good and bad, help us create this gut instinct—that is, what we feel when we know something is wrong or right based on past experiences. We tend to lean on it and it helps us make those significant decisions later in life. A lifetime of valued lessons shapes your hunch.

How often do we not trust our instincts, though? How often do you talk yourself out of the right decision? I knew before my former marriage that something wasn't 'right', but I didn't listen to myself. I didn't trust my hunch.

Despite the differences between my former spouse and I, I convinced myself that everything was perfect. We clearly had different expectations about our careers, and we constantly challenged each other over finances, our commitment to the relationship and more. Although neither of us was wrong, we didn't agree on the same path yet still forced a marriage.

You can probably relate to this. Have you ever made a decision but later regretted it? You knew you shouldn't have stayed in the relationship or a job, but you had too much emotional investment. What stress did this cause you, as a result?

If you want to redefine yourself, you must examine all areas of your life that affect your happiness. While you will make imperfect decisions, understand why and how they occurred. You may find that they could've been avoided simply by trusting your gut.

While it may help you with significant decisions, rationality can help you decide on the small things in life, like choosing products at a supermarket. With good reason and evaluation, you can make appropriate decisions based on your wants and needs in a short amount of time. For instance, when you select a loaf of bread, you might consider freshness, brand recognition, taste, and more. The selection process shouldn't extend beyond several minutes.

While we can consider every detail of this decision, at what point will our brain lose focus on what's most important to us? When it comes to shopping, in general, I'm always overwhelmed. I do endless research before making a decision, such as which toaster I should purchase. I analyze reviews, product comparisons, and so on until I'm overwhelmed with stress. I'll waste two to three hours researching a product that will not significantly impact my life.

According to Jonah Lehrer, author of *How We Decide*, a wealth of information creates a poverty of attention and awareness. Are you submerging your brain into a "vat of too much data" to the point that it can no longer much new information anymore? Ever wonder why phone numbers are seven digits? Our brain can only handle seven "thought items" at a time, give or take two. Like any sponge, the brain reaches a level of saturation where it can no longer pull in content (moisture), and it ends up leading to a dripping mess.

Unfortunately, the prefrontal cortex of the brain, which monitors thoughts and evaluates emotions, can be paralyzed when overloaded. What does this mean to you? That at times there might be an automatic shutdown in your brain when you need to make a decision.

Accepting and knowing what you can realistically handle at a given time is the key to minimizing stress. Seven "thought items" are hardly enough for the onslaught of processing needed in our world of rapid-fire information. You may have to be selective in what you choose to consider, and how much, when deciding on anything.

REFLECTION SECTION

1. Awareness: Describe a stressful significant decision you've made recently. What process did you utilize to reach your final decision? Also, describe a stressful minor decision you've made recently. What method did you employ to reach this final decision? Did you rely on your gut or rationality for each of these decisions?

2. Acceptance: Are you willing to accept how you handled past decisions?

3. Adaptation: How would you approach your decisions differently if you approached the same situations?

11

Control the Influence on
Your Decisions

ALTHOUGH YOU MAY BE aware of your hunch or rationality, you must also consider outside influences on your decisions.

According to Richard Thaler and Cass Sunstein, authors of the book *Nudge*, this phenomenon of "choice architecture" describes the way in which decisions and outcomes may be influenced by how the choices are presented. It is the science of structuring choice, and it surrounds you daily. Candy at the supermarket register and how one presents options when asking for a favor are just a couple of examples.

When I grocery shop, I usually become a little hungry after staring at mouth-watering food during my trip. Since I'm not going to make a homemade stew in aisle three, I occasionally throw a Snickers bar in my cart at the register for a quick snack. I love the taste of chocolate, and usually nothing seems more satisfying than gooey caramel dripping from chocolate-coated peanuts when I'm hungry. The Snickers commercials have appealed to my sugary insecurities and influenced my candy choice.

While Snickers' parent company, Mars, Inc., (and many other businesses) have invested millions into commercials in order to make me think about chocolate, an even more strategic approach takes this influence to the next level. An actual "choice architect" was hired to appeal to my impulses and hunger pangs by placing this sweet, low-cost product near the register

Your decision may be nudged in a different way, too. The presentation of options could shape your perspective and influence your final decision. For example, most things sound better when presented next to something worse. If a friend asks you to either help paint a bedroom or remove fiberglass insulation from the attic, the painting option sounds like a godsend. If the same person asks if you want instead to sweep the floors or paint a bedroom, the sweeping option probably sounds a heck of a lot sweeter. Why not paint either way? If you are basing your decision on effort and cleanliness, you will always choose the lesser task.

Most likely, you have been a victim of these nudges. These choice architects are very strategic and efficient at creating an environment space that makes it very hard for people to avoid their wants. There are also friends, family, and other random people in your life who strategically present unfavorable options without harmful intent. They are merely influencing your behavior for their advantage. It's up to you to recognize this and ask the right questions.

REFLECTION SECTION

1. Awareness: What subtle nudges lead to your less than desirable behaviors and impulsive urges?

2. Acceptance: Are you willing to accept that outside influences steer your decisions, but also that you have developed the awareness to control them in the future?

3. Adaptation: How can you control outside influences on your decisions? Are there situations you should avoid? If so, how would you do so?

12

Change Your Environment

YOU CAN TRAVEL TO the ends of the Earth to make a change within yourself, but if you're stuck in the middle of a tornado while doing so, it's a tough journey.

There is no way around it: your environment affects you. It may also shape you. When you're trying to redefine yourself, you can't just ignore it if you feel hopeless view your life and the world negatively, or repeatedly place yourself in adverse situations—your unhappiness may be the result of reasons outside of yourself.

I can't help but think of childhood development when discussing this topic. I'm a product of divorced parents, much like most families in the United States of Traditional Families. I would be lying if I said that seeing my parents argue didn't shape how I communicated (I almost wrote, "argued") in future relationships. I was a sponge in a stressful environment!

All things considered, I'm fortunate that I experienced a great childhood in a safe home with plenty of positive influences. Other children aren't as lucky. Countless studies have shown the adverse long-term adverse of abusive parents and constant conflict on children. The constant exposure to this type of environment can emotionally, mentally, and physically scar them. In many cases, the children replicate the same abusive behavior as adults.

This environment is most familiar to them and can consequently shape their behaviors and perspectives. A child with less access to resources to live in his or her home may develop fears related to survival that many children in middle to upper-income households never fathom. It's hard to feel great about life when you're in a negative environment that barely meets your basic survival needs.

You might say, "I'm not little orphan Annie though—that's not me." You may be right. Nevertheless, you are still influenced by your environment as an adult, and you may not always realize it. A smile from a friend means more to you than you recognize. After identifying a smile, the mirror neurons in the frontal lobe of your brain light up as if you were smiling yourself. You are reaping the same benefits of internal euphoria that you experience when you're happy just by looking at another smiling face.

This biological response has intriguing implications when we contemplate change. Since your ultimate goal is happiness, this means you can increase it by biologically feeding off of other people's physical positivity!

Although you intend to surround yourself with positive energy, it's difficult to avoid the constant bombardment of negative political banter on the radio, violent images on television and film, and complaints about miserable work and home conditions from friends, family, and co-workers. These external influences may overtake your mind whether they're welcome or not. Unknowingly, the negative messages and images might be reinforced enough that your unconscious will eventually play the same 'album' on repeat. Consequently, you may be the next person with an undermining negative inner voice that speaks up while in the shower (like in Tim's story from earlier).

Have you ever thought about how much negativity surrounds

you? Think about the dialogue in your social circles. What emotions do you notice? Are people constantly negative or complaining? Do you converse the same way?

Think about the shows and movies that you watch. What images and messages are you seeing? Do those themes influence your behaviors, feelings, or even your dreams in any way?

Think about everyone that you see daily. Are those people happy? Or are they "going through the motions" of life?

If you take a look around, you'll probably notice that most people are unhappy. Unfortunately, most people recognize it and do very little to change it. Their perception is commonly one of, "it is what it is."

Our world is full of naysayers and negative banter. Who would possibly be motivated to do anything when they feel helpless and a lack of control?

Even if you feel a sense of control, there are plenty of reasons why you wouldn't change your environment. Your work environment may be plagued with constant gossip and complaining, but you're not going to quit because you depend on the income. Your home environment may be plagued with an unhappy marriage, a constant struggle to make ends meet in a space too small for two young kids, but you're not going to divorce your spouse and abandon your children.

Do you believe that you should accept "it is what it is", though? If you recognize how your environment affects you, shouldn't you take the time to reshape it? Now is the time:

- To examine the relationship you have with your environment.
- To walk away from negative conversations or change the subject.
- To look at your perceptions and question their roots.
- To simplify your marriage or relationship and create a foundation of selflessness.
- To use positive messages to counter the repetitive negative messages.

REFLECTION SECTION

1. Awareness: How does your environment affect your attitude
    and perspective? What negative or destructive influences do
    you notice? What particular radio, film, television, and print
    messages negatively affect your behavior and how?

2. Acceptance: Are you willing to accept that you can't change your environment at this moment, but you can adapt it to the future?

3. Adaptation: How can you control the negative and destructive influences in your environment? Describe three strategies that you will utilize to control these forces in your personal and professional lives and create a positive environment.

13

Approach New Problems
With Confidence

BEYOND YOUR DECISION-MAKING APPROACH, it is necessary to examine other mental processes, too. Your problem-solving approach is the most underestimated of these processes and can cause a significant amount of stress. How often do you recognize a problem and then haphazardly take a leap of faith? You may take this step more often than you'd like to admit or know.

Most likely, the root of your stress isn't the result of the solution you choose, but instead the approach you took to reach it and your level of patience. Problems will demand different levels of consideration and analysis, but each will need at least a minute of attention. Using an adapted version of a problem-solving approach from the book *The Cognitive-Behavioral Treatment of Obesity* by Zafra Cooper, you should identify a problem accurately and specifically; consider multiples solutions and their implications; then choose the best solution and act upon it.

First, Cooper states that you should, "identify the problem as early as possible," and then "specify the problem accurately" in his process. We don't need reminders, though, to identify a problem as early as possible. If you're aware, you identify the problem as early as you can—nothing more than that.

The following are examples of this step in your problem-solving approach.

DISHES SCENARIO

Problem:
My husband leaves dishes in the sink.

Your reactive assumption, without breaking down the problem:
That selfish idiot leaves dishes in the sink every day for me!

Accurately and specifically breaking down the problem:
I've noticed that he has been leaving dishes in the sink on Mondays and Thursdays after breakfast.

Breakdown:
Interesting. It's amazing how often we jump to wrongful, emotionally-driven assumptions when we first notice a problem. What a state of stress for everyone involved! You blame your poor husband for everything!

I've been guilty of this "jumping of the gun" attitude and have been quickly reminded to slow down and reexamine the situation. In our situation, Mr. Dishes is guilty of leaving dishes, but upon further dissection, it's not every day. Most important, you've reacted without considering why he might be doing this or how a simple solution can rectify the problem.

DATING SCENARIO

Problem:
I've been on at least one date per week for six months, and none has led to a successful relationship!

Your reactive assumptions without breaking down the problem:
There are no good-looking, unmarried guys left! Nobody wants to go on more than one date with me, and I'll be alone for the rest of my life! Not only that, but my butt looks fat in these jeans! Ughhhhhhhhhh!

Accurately and specifically breaking down the problem:
After six months of going on dates with different guys that you met at bars, you have gone on more than one date with only three of them. Although they were good-looking (and unmarried!), you later found that they weren't compatible with you.

Breakdown:
In our second scenario, your dating life is the focus. After six months, you're still disappointed that you're not in a long-term relationship with someone. You perceive this as a problem. Again, it's easy to jump to your emotional or irrational state. Unfortunately, this reaction can lead to unfair stress about men's interest in you and your physical attributes.

Most times, if you begin to break down the problem accurately and specifically, you'll see (just as we do, in this case) that our initial perceptions are not always the most accurate. Yes, you are still single, but you have still met a few good-looking men that have led to more than one date. This can be seen as a positive and a sign that you're on the right track.

If you want the best solution to a problem, it starts with a reasonable, accurate, and specific interpretation of its roots, which involves monitoring your emotions at the same time. There are many situations that are unfortunate and may lead to feelings of grief, despair, and more. Should you push these feelings deep into your unconscious and just move forward? More times than not, these situations are evoking emotion for a reason, and you shouldn't just ignore or reject these feelings.

Instead, take the time to understand how this challenge affects you and try not to dwell on it. A problem requires a thorough examination of its parts and the implications of multiple solutions. Once you accept that the world isn't perfect, you choose the best solution and then act.

You will want to find the solution that will lead to the most happiness and the least amount of stress. This may require you to brainstorm and lay out a variety of options ranging from obscure to familiar.

When you develop a list of your possible solutions, you are taking a step in the right direction. The solutions are only as valuable as knowing their implications, though. This action evokes a greater thought process and can require creative ideas outside of your own.

If I'm unwilling to examine what I don't know or haven't seen, my creativity is limited. You may fall into this category. I NEED to learn about the approaches that other people have taken to resolve the same problem. Sometimes their solution can be applied directly to my issue or trigger the right idea for a new one. A simple outside opinion about my problem could offer the same value. Explore the solutions and their implications that you know, but never discount the value of the ideas that lie outside of yourself. They may trigger a more successful solution than you ever imagined.

In our Dishes and Dating Scenarios, let's examine different solutions for each.

DISHES SCENARIO

Solutions/Implications

Solution:
Constantly watch your husband and continue to follow him until he finishes the dishes.

Implication:
Yes, your husband may wash the dishes, but he is only doing so because he is incredibly annoyed that you're following him. Not only that, but you are now neglecting your own responsibilities. You shouldn't be wasting your time following your husband.

Solution:
Find out if your husband is overwhelmed with work and accept the responsibility of dishwashing if so.

Implication:
It's possible that the stress of work will affect his participation at home. If you accept this responsibility, you will relieve a burden in his day. In the long term, though, you value a partnership and equal participation at home, and this may not be the best solution.

Solution:
Learn why your husband has been leaving dishes, express how important maintaining a clean house is to you and ask your husband to contribute in other productive ways that are more enjoyable to him.

Implication:
Again, it's important to understand the reasons for your husband's actions. They may be unintentional, or he just hates washing dishes (when he would gladly do anything else). In a relationship, communication is necessary, and this is an opportunity to discuss how each of you can contribute. Overall, you are encouraging him to

take ownership over a responsibility that he's more likely to complete, and are at least giving him an opportunity to explain himself.

DATING SCENARIO

Solutions/Implications

Solution:
Explore online dating.
Implication:
Online dating will open the door to new options. You can meet interesting and different people that you may never encounter otherwise. On the other hand, you don't know someone until you meet them in person, and blind dates are especially hit or miss.

Solution:
Find out if your friends have single friends.
Implication:
You enjoy the company of your friends and may adore the companionship of their likeminded single friends, too. Similar to online dating, you can meet interesting and different people that you may never encounter otherwise. On the other hand, you don't know someone until you meet them in person, and blind dates are especially hit or miss.

Solution:
Continue to date people you meet at bars.
Implication:
You've done this for the last six months and have met a few people worthy of more than one date. This solution has already proven some level of success. On the other hand, meeting people when they're out drinking can be a toss-up, and you haven't met a long-term boyfriend yet.

Despite this expansive list of solutions, you may not feel complete satisfaction with any one choice. In fact, it may feel like a loss. Additionally, the solution you choose may not lead to success. While there is rarely a perfect path, look at a problem with the most scrupulous eye and decide on the most reasonable solution. Do what you can, and accept this decision (the solution). If you must, return to your list of solutions and attempt a different one.

In our scenarios, a single solution (like option three in the Dishes Scenario) is most ideal. Sometimes, however, the one solution is really the integration of many (as we saw in the Dating Scenario). Let's take a look:

DISHES SCENARIO

Best Solution:
Do you really want to follow your husband around the house? I certainly hope not—life is far more valuable than that. You'll always find solutions that might work as well as the rest (like #2), but you want to be sure it will be the best long-term fit for you. If a partnership is what you value most, it looks like you found a solution (#3) that is most respectful to both parties.

DATING SCENARIO

Best Solution:
In this scenario, several factors make your final decision tough. The solutions share the idea that you don't really know someone until you meet them in person.

Meanwhile, you can argue that each solution presents a drawback as well as a positive reason. With this in mind, it may be in your best interest to employ every solution. Individually, the solutions may not help you. Collectively, the solutions may place you on the path of companionship.

No matter the situation, there is a point where you have to choose and then act. No problem is left unattended, and each will require a decision even if it means you avoid temporarily making one.

Your strength as a person lies in your approach to life's challenges—not your successes or failures. We already know that life isn't perfect. It's up to you shape a life in which you can emotionally handle and carry out a solution to the best of your best ability.

REFLECTION SECTION

1. Awareness: Describe two recent problems. How did you approach each problem? Were you satisfied with the outcome?

2. Acceptance: Are you willing to accept the responsibility to approach every problem with patience and due diligence? Will you accept the outcome of the chosen solution?

3. Adaptation: Use the adapted Cooper's problem-solving approach to reexamine your two recent problems.

    •   Identify the problem accurately and specifically

    •   Consider as many solutions as possible and their implications

    •   Choose the best solution and then act

14

Accumulate Wisdom Through Error

WE ACCUMULATE WISDOM THROUGH introspection, analysis of our self and our environment, and an open-minded inspection of the errors we make and why.

Every once in a while, you need to reflect on and evaluate your actions and perspectives. You need regular check-ins to examine your little or big hiccups along the way. Are you a creature of habit making the same mistakes over and over? Do you mismanage your time? Do you misconfigure your finances monthly? Do you place yourself in the same type of destructive relationships repeatedly?

If you continue to make the same mistakes, you probably shouldn't allow yourself off the hook. Nevertheless, making mistakes is part of the learning process and sometimes we have to make them repeatedly before we notice they're a problem. Exploring, making mistakes, and then succeeding are substantial tenants to learning.

With that being said, the advice of "Make a mistake! It'll be worth it!" contradicts most teachings in our rigid, perfectionistic world. Although your peers may view your mistakes as failures, I'm giving you the permission to mess up! Take the burden of perfection off of your shoulders. Live freely!

There's one caveat, however. Many people have studied history, yet still repeat the same mistakes. Unlike them, you will LEARN from your mistakes. The only way you can change this trend is to accept your mistake and examine why you continue to repeat the same error.

Your ability to accept your mistakes will determine your success. Don't allow yourself to dwell on a past that you can't change. Accept the failure of your initial approach and then develop a new adaptive strategy. You may find that this error can help you with your process of elimination and trigger an idea for a new direction.

Once you accept a particular mistake, you must examine the path to a solution. Did an insecurity or fear steer you to make the mistake? Was your environment pressuring you to take a less-desirable approach? Did you then identify the problem accurately? Did you consider all of the possible solutions?

Simplify the parts of any error, face them, and employ your new problem-solving approach. You may not always resolve the error entirely, but you may develop the building blocks for a strategy that will help overcome parts of it.

REFLECTION SECTION

1. Awareness: Describe two significant mistakes that you struggled to accept over the last year. How did facing these errors
    make you feel? What is the root of each of mistake?

2. Acceptance: Are you willing to accept that the mistakes are in the past?

3. Adaptation: Utilize the adapted Cooper's problem-solving approach to avoid these errors again.

   • Identify the problem accurately and specifically

   • Consider as many solutions as possible and their implications

   • Choose the best solution and then act

15

Create New Habits

IF YOU WANT CHANGE to stick, it needs to become a habit.

Habits are highly ingrained, learned behaviors. They are your subconscious' autopilot reaction. In a Duke University study, researchers found that 40% of our daily actions are habits. Your brain loves to multitask and will do everything in its power to build an association (consciously or otherwise). It wants to run on autopilot so that it can do the million other things it needs to do.

More times than not, your subconscious puts your keys in the same place and help you drive your proverbial car in the constant rush of your life. Habits are essentially the underlying force of your routines and take very little effort to carryout. They maintain the order in your life!

What if they are destructive, though? What if you recognize these bad habits and try to change them, but repeatedly fail? What if you want to lose weight but still grab a snack before bed like you normally do?

I wish we could just start a new routine and call it quits on the bad habit. Since the brain depends on repeated occurrences—or the value of the routines and rewards—a process must take place before this change occurs. The brain needs to know that a new habit is equally or more important.

A habit is a mental sequence that must be triggered to start. The brain must recognize a cue—an environmental signal for action based on repeated occurrences. It doesn't want to waste its time on routines that won't lead to rewards. It builds an association between a cue and helps develop a routine in hopes of a predictable reward.

If carried out repeatedly, the strength of a bad habit is probably too powerful to be extinguished quickly. You may figure out the cue to this habit and still succumb to the same destructive habit. It takes practice and your brain must be taught a new connection between the cue, the routine, and the reward. The mind doesn't want to lose its prized reward, and it will keep leading you back to what it knows best—your habit!

How do you change something so ingrained that it happens subconsciously, and that will try to undermine your individual efforts to alter it?

The answer lies in the cue and reward. Most people try to erase the whole formula and completely remove themselves from the habit (and not just the bad routine).

Unfortunately, the reward and cue are too ingrained in us to simply extinguish instantly. Even if we try to escape it, there may always be something in our environment that triggers our routine. After all, we want our reward!

In the book *The Power of Habit*, the author Charles Duhigg wonderfully illustrates our need to trick ourselves into new habits. Remember metacognition? We need to think about our thinking to keep ourselves in check. When we change our habits, we must become the Wizard of OZ and unnoticeably make minor modifications behind our unconscious "back."

We need to insert a new routine, keep the old cue, and deliver the old reward.

For example:

You lose your focus at work every day at 3 p.m. You usually have stared at your computer screen for the last two hours and the words are starting to look like alphabet soup.

At that point, you get up and walk to the office kitchen where you indulge in the morning's leftover donuts (even though you're not hungry). You've done this for two years, and now you're ten pounds heavier. In the wake of New Year's Eve, you are ready to shake off the weight. Despite your best efforts, your 3 p.m. walk to the kitchen doesn't change.

In this example, you need to break down the formula for your donut-to-mouth habit:

3 p.m. + Go to the kitchen and grab the donut that will make you overweight = Break from work

(Cue) + (Routine) = (Reward)

Take notice that the real reward is the break from work, not stuffing yourself because you're hungry (since you just ate lunch two hours ago).

In our example, we need to change the routine of going to the kitchen as our first step. You can decide to work through your 3 p.m. break, but you and I both know that you would stare at the clock for an hour thinking about that donut.

Keep your break. Instead of eating, though, visit a colleague and discuss the latest episode of your favorite show or that football game. Sit in another part of the office and read a magazine. Do whatever you want—besides eating—to give yourself the real reward: a break from your tedious work.

Repeat this sequence until you don't notice anymore. At first, it will be a fight with your subconscious to go the kitchen. You must resist. Remind yourself that you're not hungry and that you just want a break. Find something else to do.

Although the results may vary, don't be discouraged. Your self-talk will override your old, bad habits eventually. As you unravel these habits, you will create new ones by introducing new approaches to life.

REFLECTION SECTION

1. Awareness: Describe a habit you want to change. How does this habit affect you? What are the benefits of changing this habit? What are the obstacles to changing this habit?

2. Acceptance: Can you accept that you're not perfect and that it will take time, effort, and patience to change this habit?

3. Adaptation: How will you change the present routine to achieve your goal? Break down your habit into the following parts (use the donut example as a reference).

   • Cue:

   • Routine:

   • Reward:

16

Redefine Your Boundaries

I THINK IT'S SYMBOLIC of our true human nature to want to push our boundaries. We have a knack for pushing the limits.

It's the kid inside of us that still touches the oven after our mother tells us not to turn the knob. It's the "let's see if we can get away with a little more" syndrome. With this in mind, we occasionally need to protect ourselves from, well, ourselves, and define the most appropriate boundaries.

When redefining yourself, it's very easy to tell you to live a perfect life, and then you'll achieve ultimate happiness. You'll be safer if you drive the speed limit all the time. You'd reach your ideal weight if you eat just a little bit less than you normally do. Unfortunately, we have too many distractions in life and also enjoy the freedom of doing what we want.

Instead of the all or nothing approach, I employ the following analogy as a way a life. I found through trial and error that I don't receive tickets when I drive no more than nine miles per hour over the speed limit. How fast can I drive without getting a ticket? Nine seems to be the answer for where I live.

Once I hit ten, though, it's a different story. Many police officers consider speeds of ten miles per hour or more over the speed limit more dangerous, and you are more likely to receive a ticket. There is a legitimate reason for this assumption. The state has determined the speed limit for a particular road as the most ideal based on the conditions. As you speed further from this number, the likelihood of an accident increases. For this reason, the court system assigns higher penalties for this class of ticket.

I'm taking a risk by acting beyond these limits, but I'm also mindful of an appropriate boundary. I refer to this behavior as "living in the gray." You may say, "But I don't want live by any boundaries or a rule system!" Although many books will sell the idea of life without rules, it isn't possible. All of us need boundaries or a rule system. Without them, we would probably harm ourselves or others.

Besides, you already live by a set of boundaries and rules. Now you only need to redefine them. Would you eat a piece of candy lying on the wet alley pavement? Let's assume you and everyone else wouldn't. You have established this rule about food as a safety precaution.

The behavior of my weight loss clients is another example. Their weight always tends to fluctuate between the same high and low numbers. It's as if they retreat to their old habits once they reach a particular weight loss low. We learn that these figures are their tramlines, or boundaries, for their weight. Unconsciously, my clients modify their behavior when they reach a specific high or low number, for better or worse. These boundaries mark their patterns of behavior, and the tramlines must be redefined in order to achieve a healthy weight range.

What is your rule system? Is it good for you? Are you a healthier person physically, mentally, and emotionally for it? If your system and behaviors aren't in line with what you need, there's a chance you're causing yourself stress. It should be in line with your home-ostasis—your philosophical, efficient state of being. It's whatever you do for your mind and body that make it work best. If you don't know what this perfect state of being is for you, then you're living a life of chance, pushing random boundaries. Any choice you make is a risk.

From the very beginning of this book, you have been learning about YOU. Now, you must stop choosing boundaries that work for someone else and begin determining what works for your own body and mind. It doesn't matter if it works for someone else. It doesn't mean it will work for you.

When you know yourself well enough, you deserve the occasional slack to live a life outside the strict daily regiment. Disregard the teachings of many popular philosophers, pundits, and anyone else that has thrown their opinion at you. They may tell you to live this way or that way. But no matter what they say, you need to determine your boundaries based on what you discover about YOU. There isn't a perfect way to live, after all.

I greatly encourage you to "live in the gray" a little bit. It will lead to valuable lessons about your spirit. Never forget, though, that you need to base your new boundaries on your needs instead of your wants. Test your limits but keep your true self in mind. You'll be thankful when you KNOW why your weight increased, why your spouse is upset with you, or why you received a speeding ticket.

REFLECTION SECTION

1. Awareness: Describe three boundaries that guide your behaviors. How risky are these boundaries? Do they cause you more stress than good?

2. Acceptance: Are you willing to accept that these boundaries may not be in line with your pursuit of your goals and happiness? Will you redefine these boundaries?

3. Adaptation: What new boundaries would you like to create and why? What new habits will you create to maintain these new boundaries? Break down your habit into the following parts (again using the donut example from Chapter 15 as a reference).

   • Cue:

   • Routine:

   • Reward:

17

Create Conversations
With Others

THE ESSENCE OF BEING exists through the interaction with others and your environment. It's up to you to open the doors of wisdom through new conversations to get you one step closer to healthier relationships and a happier environment.

Do you want the best out of life? Of course, you do! It takes more than just listening to your internal banter. We should never forget who else we can learn from—everybody! In fact, our lives depend on it. We need interaction! We thrive on it.

Unfortunately, in the speed of life, we've lost focus on genuine interactions with people. In a constant rush to fulfill our demanding professional and personal lives, we distract ourselves from the most important spoken exchanges that often stimulate creativity, introspection, and values.

Anytime I face a challenge I always seek out the advice of friends and family. During my divorce, I wasn't sure how to handle the situation. I needed suggestions on the best path and the solutions I should consider during this emotional period of my life. Although I didn't agree with every opinion, every conversation strengthened my support system and gave me confidence while trying to determine an ideal approach. Also, the support and feedback from friends and family helped me look at myself objectively. Their insight was valuable at a fragile time.

You may also benefit from similar conversations as you face life. When you approach a challenge, a friend could help you consider new solutions. When you celebrate a moment, a family member could help you heighten the experience by sharing it with you.

You have to take the initiative to create real, meaningful conversations, however. Technology has limited our communication, and we grow further apart with every technological advancement. Phone calls have become emails. Conversations are one or two-word text messages with smiley faces.

You must take the time and effort to converse face-to-face with people. When you don't make this a priority, it's a reflection of your constant flow from one thing to the next. You're attached to an endless insignificant list, or to results in your unrelenting pursuit to complete something. It's time to redefine this pattern.

REFLECTION SECTION

1. Awareness: How often do you create conversations with people daily? Are you too preoccupied with a list of responsibilities or distracted to begin a new conversation? How often do you vocally connect with friends and family? If rarely, what obstructs you from doing so?

2. Acceptance: Can you accept your role in creating conversations?

3. Adaptation: Describe two ways you can create conversations with friends and family more often. Describe two ways you can create new conversations with people you don't know.

18

Define Your Purpose

IN A BUSINESS PLAN, we can build a structure and develop a marketing strategy but it doesn't make sense if we never define the mission statement. What is your intent? Who is your audience?

Now is the time for you to think about your own mission statement—your purpose. It's the underlying theme of you. It guides your behavior and reminds you when you're steering away from it. It isn't always perfect and is continually redefined based on your experiences.

Religious, family, societal, or personal values may define your purpose. No matter the root, though, YOU choose it. It will steer how you adapt, how you decide, how you treat others, how far you extend your boundaries, how you interact, and how you participate in the world.

The first time my friend Jenny asked me about my purpose I was speechless. I didn't know what my purpose was, and it showed. I reflected on my life and realized how aimlessly I lived. Most experiences were just a collection of random instances that collided to create my life. Relationship. Career. Everything. It was missing a linear connection.

It only took a little investigating to learn what steered me: My interactions with people. I realized that my purpose was to guide people in their efforts to understand themselves and the world. *Redefine Yourself* embodies this intent, and I will continue to live my life with it in mind.

Have you thought about your purpose? We haven't approached this question yet for good reason. You can't build a shelter in a tornado. There was no sense in encouraging you to write a personal mission statement in an emotional funnel when you just want to find sanity outside of the storm. You can't build a new you without the storm clearing your self-obstacles first. You need a clear vision of yourself and your direction.

Now, after countless hours of introspection and the repetitive messages in this book, you are starting to part the clouds. Determine your purpose, but be sure it's reflective of you. You don't have to be anyone you're not, and you don't have to be the person who does it all.

My great friend, Craig, shared an insight years back about volunteering. In high school, Craig volunteered at a nursing home and spent his afternoons listening to the stories of lonely seniors. With consideration of his volunteering spirit, I requested his participation in my food drive. With genuine assertiveness, Craig said, "No."

He told me that he loves to volunteer but only prefers to work with seniors. Craig is one of the most genuine people I know, and he doesn't have to help everyone. He's entitled to choose to live in a way that serves his purpose.

I keep this story in mind as I live my life and you should, too. Think about your purpose, but never feel obligated to extend yourself in a way that steers you from happiness.

REFLECTION SECTION

1. Awareness: Have you ever thought about your purpose? What are you passionate about in your life? What is your mission statement?

2. Acceptance: Will you accept that you may need to identify your purpose and redefine how you live your life in order to achieve it?

3. Adaptation: Describe your purpose in a sentence or two. Reflect on your experiences. What will your legacy be? What should steer your behaviors and perspectives?

19

Create Goals to Maintain Your Positive Focus

IT'S EASY TO BE distracted by the nonsense of life. Besides our purpose, we need other day-to-day, positive focuses in order to maintain a healthy and happy perspective. A list of goals may bring you the positive direction you need.

I realized a couple of years ago that I needed a new focus after my divorce. When married, I felt like I was living a 'status quo' life. I rarely pursued the things I wanted nor did I make an effort to achieve them. I felt unfulfilled in life. What was holding me back? Me.

You've heard my story, and you probably realize by now that I was my own worst enemy. Don't let this happen to you. Think about your life and what's missing. What have you always wanted to be? What have you always wanted to accomplish? Where have you always wanted to travel? What have you always wanted to see?

With my clean start, I created a bucket list. It helps me focus on what I want to accomplish, experience and see before I die.

Make your own list, too. Don't waste your time like I did, continually putting off the things you want the most. Don't sit back and watch life pass you by anymore. As you complete specific items, replace them with something else. This list will evolve as you progress through life.

Where do you start? By stealing my list! Use my list as an example and start experiencing the life you want most.

- Vacation in an igloo village in Finland.
- Set foot on all seven continents.
- ~~Sip espresso in a café in Italy with Sammy while peering over the ancient ruins of Rome~~ (completed in the fall of 2014).
- ~~Write a book~~ (completed in 2015).
- Learn how to swim well.
- Learn how to dance without thinking.
- Be paid for what I love talking about the most (my book).
- Attend the Olympic Games.
- Ride a hot air balloon in Egypt.
- Ride on the Singapore Flyer, the second-tallest Ferris wheel in the world.
- ~~Ride on a Ggondola in Venice, Italy~~ (completed in the fall of 2014).
- Go on a safari in the Maasai Mara National Reserve in Kenya.
- Bathe in the Blue Lagoon Geothermal Spa, a massive geothermal pool inside a lava field in Grindavik, Iceland.
- Visit Machu Picchu, the lost city of the Incas.
- Swim with dolphins.
- ~~Visit the Eiffel Tower~~ (completed in the fall of 2014).
- Visit the White House.
- Take a helicopter tour over Kauai, Hawaii, filming location for the original movie *Jurassic Park*.
- Forgive daily and let go of grudges (eternal work in progress).
- Attend the next White Sox World Series.

- See a performance at the Sydney Opera House.
- Visit Easter Island.
- Visit Patagonia in South America.
- Reach the top 20 in Amazon self-improvement book sales.
- Marry Sammy.
- Raise children.
- Volunteer for at least two hours per week.

REFLECTION SECTION

1. Awareness: Are you living the life you want? Describe two
   goals you have always wanted to achieve. What obstacles have
   you faced while pursuing these goals? If you haven't pursued
   them, why not?

2. Acceptance: Can you accept the responsibility of creating the life you want?

3. Adaptation: Describe at least two answers for each of the following questions and start compiling your bucket list.

   • What have you always wanted to be?

   • What have you always wanted to accomplish?

   • Where have you always wanted to travel?

   • What have you always wanted to see?

20

The Next Step

I WAS SITTING IN my hair stylist's chair as she was telling me about the self-help book she just read. I think it was Stephen Covey's *The Seven Habits of Highly Effective People,* but I can't recall exactly. What was most momentous about this occasion was her remark: "I just love that book! It's the fourth time I've read it!"

I remember thinking "Lady, if you need to read that four times there's a problem here. You're clearly not getting it." The more I thought about it, though, I realized that I was the one not getting it.

Information regarding the direction of our lives streams at us from the media non-stop. These constant messages send us into a confusing tailspin. When we finally approach what we think is the right message, it's replaced by the next one.

With that being said, if you want REAL change, don't stop re-defining yourself now.

Occasionally scan through this book and review your answers. Your new life experiences may lead you to write a new business plan for yourself. After more time, check back again to see if your

NEW life is still in line. Read the book ten times if you must. Talk about it with friends and family. Convince yourself of the new you. Live the new you. Be the new you. Make this change a constant in your life.

Our real self is a complicated combination of nature and nurture. It will not just automatically change at the close of this book. If you're like most, the change will happen temporarily, and then you will retreat to your old habits, trends, and patterns. DO NOT underestimate your ability to undermine yourself.

Although this is the end of my story, this is just the beginning of yours. You have started the process of redefining yourself. Now continue this commitment to YOU and begin to live as your best self.

APPENDIX

Three Ways to Start a New Life Today

#1: Develop a routine.
The biggest contributor to a stress-free lifestyle is routine. Without it, life is chaos. It provides the foundation for all of your behaviors and gives you the consistency to reach a goal. Whether it's related to eating, sleeping or exercising, be sure to determine your needs accurately and lay out the groundwork for successful completion.

#2: Remind yourself to enjoy each day.
It's a shame we need to remind ourselves to enjoy each day. Over the last ten years, I've learned from my personal training clients that people are generally unhappy. I don't blame them. With the overwhelming stresses of work, family, and Chicago sports, it's easy to be distracted from the fruits of life.

Although I wouldn't expect you to dismiss these stresses, I certainly encourage to change your perspective on them. Life will throw challenges at you each day. It's time to embrace them as learning experiences for growth and wisdom. By doing this, you may look at these challenges in a more positive light and begin to enjoy the process of living—not just the achievement of results.

#3: Simplify your life.

Since there are many obstacles that you face daily, simplify your approach and environment as much as possible. Life is stressful when submerged under a disorganized mess. Make the following changes today:

- Get rid of clothes, paperwork, and other random things in your closet, cabinets, trunk, yard, garage, and basement that you haven't touched in 6 months.
- Quit trying to multitask. Free your mind and focus on one thought at a time.
- Place things that you use daily in the same spot (e.g., your keys, phone, etc.). Quit wasting time searching for misplaced items.
- Consolidate bank accounts. Track your spending habits all in one place.
- Save time by ordering what you need online. You no longer need to waste hours searching for products in multiple stores.
- How long does it take you to wash your clothes? Have you thought about consolidating your whites and colors in cold water? Unless your clothes are filthy, there isn't a need to separate your clothes into different loads. Save your time, sanity, and money and wash everything at once.
- Learn to say no. Quit overextending yourself! Only accept projects, social invitations or responsibilities within your limits.
- Unsubscribe to email newsletters.

Remember This Script While
You Redefine Yourself

Today, I will be my best self.

I will reach new heights.

I will make changes when necessary…and not just on New Year's Day.

I will be positive every day.

I will travel more.

I will make a difference in someone's life.

I will define my natural boundaries.

I will believe in myself.

I will only judge myself fairly and with an open mind.

I will be bigger than the moment.

I will be aware of my surroundings.

I will control my impulses.

I will manage my emotions.

I will build my best physical self.

I will love unconditionally.

I will listen and seek understanding.

I will only judge people fairly with an open mind.
I will volunteer.
I will choose to live.
I will make my life a great story.
I will be my best self.

Charitable Organizations I Support

As you redefine your purpose, think about the people in your community in need of your help. Although I've provided a list of organizations that would love your support, I encourage you to find one in your community that you're passionate about.

Gilda's Club Chicago

All of us have been affected by cancer through family members, friends, or co-workers. Gilda's Club is a place where men, women, and children whose lives have been touched by cancer, as well as their families and friends, can feel they are part of a supporting community. Their innovative program offers various support programs at their clubhouse and many hospitals across the United States and is an essential complement to medical care.

I'm grateful for the time I spent on the associate board of Gilda's Club Chicago, and I encourage you to volunteer your time as well. Learn more about them on their website gildasclubchicago.org or visit a clubhouse in your city.

Compass to Care

Compass to Care ensures that all families can access life-saving cancer treatment for their children. They carry out this mission by scheduling and paying for travel arrangements to the hospital where a child is being treated for cancer. Ultimately, Compass to Care gives children the best access to life-saving cancer treatment, regardless of their family's financial situation. Learn more about them on their website compasstocare.org.

National Runaway Safeline

The National Runaway Safeline helps keep America's runaway, homeless, and at-risk youth safe and off the streets. It's our responsibility to provide the best for our youth, but, unfortunately, many children are victims of unfortunate circumstances and lack the resources they need to thrive. Find out how you can help by visiting 1800runaway.org.

Reach Out and Read Illinois

Reach Out and Read Illinois is an evidence-based nonprofit organization of medical providers who promote early literacy and school readiness in pediatric exam rooms statewide by integrating children's books and advice to parents about the importance of reading aloud into well-child visits. Learn more about them on their website reachoutandread.org.

Additional Reading

How to Win Friends and Influence People by Dale Carnegie
I've always enjoyed the relatable storytelling and writing style of Dale Carnegie. He wrote this book in 1936 and its principles for building strong relationships still appeal today. The book inspires me to be genuinely interested in other people; to be a good listener; refrain from criticizing, condemning or complaining; to give honest and sincere appreciation; and to smile. Although the book is popular in corporate circles, its message applies to all personal relationships, too.

Don't Sweat the Small Stuff...and It's All Small Stuff by Richard Carlson
Carlson's book is an easy-to-read guide on how to live with random, positive anecdotes thrown in. It was my first self-help book and has been a fixture on my bookshelf for over 18 years. As I wrote *Redefine Yourself*, I always kept it in mind.

The Power of Habit: Why We Do What We Do in Life and Business by Charles Duhigg

While Chapter 16 (Create New Habits) gives you some simple tools for change, *The Power of Habit* provides more insight on the creation of habits and how they rule our lives. The stories are interesting and make for a quick read.

How We Decide by Jonah Lehrer

Lehrer explores the neuroscience of our decision-making processes in this book. Don't be intimidated by the research and references to anatomy—his writing style is appealing, enjoyable, and the insight fascinating. Lehrer's explanation of mirror neurons will continue to resonate within me for a long time. If you're interested in how our brain operates, you'll want to add *How We Decide* to your book collection.

Imagine: How Creativity Works by Jonah Lehrer

Imagine is less technical than Lehrer's earlier work, How We Decide. It steers my approach to creativity within my business. If you haven't heard the creation story of the "Just Do It" slogan, you may want to read this today. It will change the way you approach any creative project.

The 4-Hour Workweek by Timothy Ferriss

Ferriss' book on how to minimize life's distractions and maximize efficiency in order to live more and work less may help you rethink your approach to life. If you can put aside some of his questionable marketing techniques, his tips and stories can help you create a more efficient life, both personally and professionally. I read the book at a time when I needed a push to finally do what I wanted most—it may influence you the same way.

Drive by Daniel H. Pink

In *Drive*, Pink explores the role of motivation and purpose in both the classroom and the workplace. Without a doubt, it greatly influenced the chapters on control and purpose in this book, and I highly recommend Pink's work for additional insight on these topics.

In Defense of Food by Michael Pollan

Michael Pollan is one of the leaders of the new nutrition movement. He appears in many documentaries about the food industry and is considered an expert in natural eating habits. *In Defense of Food* revolutionized my nutritional approach and changed the way I look at food. If you want to redefine the way you eat, this book is the perfect place to start.

Why Zebras Don't Get Ulcers by Robert Sapolsky

Sapolsky lightly spins humor with academic research in this book about anatomy and stress. *Why Zebras Don't Get Ulcers* has shaped my perspective on the body and stress.

Bibliography

Carlson, Richard Ph. D. Don't Sweat the Small Stuff. N.p.: Thorndyke., n.d. Print.

Carnegie, Dale. How to Win Friends and Influence People. New York: Simon and Schuster, 1981. Print.

Cooper, Zafra. Cognitive Behavioral Treatment for Obesity: A Clinician's Guide. N.p.: Guilford, 2004. Print.

Douglass, Frederick. Autobiographies: Narrative of the Life of Frederick Douglass, an American Slave; My Bondage and My Freedom; Life and times of Frederick Douglass. New York: Literary Classics of the United States, 1994. Print.

Duhigg, Charles. The Power of Habit: Why We Do What We Do in Life and Business. New York: Random House, 2012. Print.

Ferriss, Timothy. The 4-hour Workweek: Escape 9-5, Live Anywhere, and Join the New Rich. New York: Crown, 2007. Print.

Fuhrman, Joel. Eat to Live: The Amazing Nutrient-rich Program for Fast and Sustained Weight Loss. New York: Little, Brown, 2011. Print.

Gunaratana, Henepola. Mindfulness in Plain English. Boston: Wisdom Publications, 2002. Print.

Lehrer, Jonah. How We Decide. Boston: Houghton Mifflin Harcourt, 2009. Print.

Lehrer, Jonah. Imagine: How Creativity Works. Boston: Houghton Mifflin Harcourt, 2012. Print.

Pink, Daniel H. Drive: The Surprising Truth about What Motivates Us. New York, NY: Riverhead, 2009. Print.

Pollan, Michael. In Defense of Food: An Eater's Manifesto. New York: Penguin, 2008. Print.

Sapolsky, Robert M. Why Zebras Don't Get Ulcers: A Guide to Stress, Stress Related Diseases, and Coping. New York: W.H. Freeman, 1994. Print.

Thaler, Richard H., and Cass R. Sunstein. Nudge: Improving Decisions about Health, Wealth, and Happiness. New Haven, CT: Yale UP, 2008. Print.

Become Part of the Redefine Yourself Community

You can join the Redefine Yourself community in many ways. Search for **Michael Moody Fitness** on Facebook, Instagram, and LinkedIn or tweet me at @MichaelMoodyFit.

Inspire other readers by posting a photo of how you've redefined yourself on michaelmoodyfitness.com/redefineyourself or by sharing your story in a review on Amazon or another bookseller site.

43233182R00094

Made in the USA
Lexington, KY
22 July 2015